"Everyone over age 50 who is interested in creative and vital pursuits should rush to his or her nearest bookstore and buy Albert Myers' new book, Blueprint for Success.*"*
—Edith Vierck, Consulting Analyst
to the U.S. Senate Special Committee on Aging
and author of *Choices and Challenges*

*"*Blueprint for Success *is must reading for anyone like me who is changing directions in life. Albert Myers is a brilliant and inspiring author. He proves without a doubt that, with proper planning and attitude, the best is yet to come."*
—Philip Winn, former Ambassador to Switzerland

"Like a pro football player, Al Myers has outlined a Game Plan on how to organize and run a small business; with over 50 years of experience, Al should know."
—Ken Dychtwald, Ph.D., author of *Age Wave*
and President of Age Wave, Inc.

"I've known Al Myers since the first quarter of the game. Al leads by example. He doesn't just talk about how to achieve success over 50, he lives it in his own life. This book is timely and will be helpful to many at a critical time in their lives."
—Lloyd Schermer, Chairman and CEO of Lee Enterprises
and Chairman of the American Newspaper
Publishers Association

"Albert Myers, in my judgment, is highly qualified to offer valuable insight and advice for starting a business. The reader, regardless of age, will find his words inspiring and extremely informative."
—Charles Percy, former U.S. Senator,
former Chairman of the Foreign Relations Committee,
current member of the Special Commission on Aging
and author of *Growing Old in the Country of the Young*

BLUEPRINT FOR SUCCESS

BLUEPRINT FOR SUCCESS

THE COMPLETE GUIDE
TO STARTING
A BUSINESS
AFTER 50

ALBERT MYERS

NEWCASTLE PUBLISHING CO., INC.
North Hollywood, California
1991

Edited by Karen Westerberg Reyes and Lorena Fletcher Farrell
Cover Design by Michele Lanci-Altomare

First Edition August 1991

A Newcastle Book
First Printing August 1991
9 8 7 6 5 4 3 2 1
Printed in the United States of America

Acknowledgments

As a result of an article about my Institute for Success Over 50 that appeared in *Parade* magazine, I received thousands of letters from people asking for detailed information about starting a business. *Blueprint for Success* is the result. I was fortunate to have the encouragement and cooperation of a number of people who know what it takes to organize, develop and maintain a successful small business. My thanks to them for sharing their wealth of information.

I owe a special debt of gratitude to Karen Reyes and Lorena Fletcher Farrell who edited this book and kept me on schedule throughout the process of its completion.

I also must thank Al Saunders, publisher of Newcastle Publishing Company; John Wood for his friendship and initial reorganization of the manuscript; and Christopher P. Anderson, co-author with me of *Success Over Sixty*, for his continued support and good counsel.

And a special word of gratitude to Greg McCombs, who has served as Executive Director of The Institute for Success Over 50 for the last four years. Without him, *Blueprint for Success* would not have been possible.

Special thanks to Ron Hume, former Senator Charles Percy, Monte Goldman, Ellen Brandt, Sherman Andelson, Lloyd Schermer, Elizabeth Vierck, former Ambassador Phillip Winn and Ken Dychtwald for their encouragement and friendship.

To my wife, Shirlee Kay-Myers, who has been my partner
through every step of completing this book.

Contents

Foreword

Today more than 60 million Americans are over the age of 50. During the next decade the Baby Boomers (those born between 1946 and 1964) will push that number to nearly a third of the total population. With life expectancies extending well into the 80s, most people will find themselves with 30 or more years ahead after they retire—and they will be years when many may decide to at last pursue their postponed dreams of starting and running their own businesses.

Blueprint for Success tells you everything you need to know about becoming a successful entrepreneur, from what types of businesses offer the best opportunities for growth to how to obtain the most favorable financing possible. The book also contains more source material (including addresses and phone numbers) than any other on the subject. More important, *Blueprint for Success* is written by a successful retiree in a very personal way. He not only tackles the nuts and bolts of businessing, but points out and tells you how to handle the emotional and psychological challenges confronting the over-50 entrepreneur.

When it comes to making the best of opportunities during the second half of one's life, Myers is his own best advertisement. He is a University of Illinois graduate who served as a Lieutenant Colonel in the U.S. Army Air Forces during World War II. He spent 40 years in the retail business before stepping down as president of

Myers Brothers Department Stores. He then founded a chain of 16 successful travel agencies, started a coal-exporting company, and launched a hot-air-balloon charter service.

In 1984, Myers co-authored with me the bestselling book *Success Over Sixty* (Summit Books). As a result of that success Myers started The Institute for Success Over 50 in Aspen, Colorado. The Institute serves as a national resource center for older Americans who seek to make the best of all the years of their lives.

—Christopher Andersen

Prologue

For an article that appeared in *Parade* magazine I was asked to list the top business choices for over-50 entrepreneurs. According to research carried out by The Institute for Success Over 50, the following seven business categories are the most popular:

- **Retail Stores** usually reflect the owner's special interest and can run the gamut from flower shops to auto-supply stores.
- **Food Businesses**, a very popular choice, include restaurants, catering services, cafés, pizzerias, doughnut shops and the like.
- **Crafts** enterprises are always desirable because they can be run from the home. What a pleasant surprise to discover that a hobby enjoyed for years can be turned into a profitmaking business.
- **Consultancies** are the natural choice for knowledgeable and retired professionals in such areas as marketing, engineering and personnel.
- **Business Services** have cropped up all over the country. Examples include secretarial services, instant printers, photocopy stores and income-tax-preparation firms.
- **Hospitality**, another ideal choice for the over-50 businessperson, includes the management of hotels, motels, bed-and-breakfast inns and travel agencies.
- **Franchises** range from candy stores to car washes to lawn-care operations, and a significant percentage of owners are over 50.

The Institute for Success Over 50 was formed to answer a need voiced by the ever-growing mature segment of the population that wants to remain active, healthy, productive—and above all, in the mainstream. The Institute has become an intregral part of this national movement. It continues to help by providing a blueprint for overcoming the psychological and emotional obstacles that stand in the way of many over-50 entrepreneurs. And it offers practical guidelines on how to best integrate a lifetime of experience and talent to ensure that the later years are the best years of one's life. These findings are reflected in *Blueprint for Success*.

Laying the Groundwork

Finding out exactly where you fit in the scheme of business is the first challenge. *Blueprint for Success* offers advice gleaned from years of work at The Institute for Success Over 50 in the following areas:

- Incorporating what you already know into structuring a new career.
- Negotiating the nuts and bolts of a new business, including structure, financing, marketing, and personnel concerns. How can you obtain credit, get the best employees, start a relationship with a bank, and set up an office?
- Assessing your risk-taking quotient. How much risk did you take to get where you are now? And how much additional risk will it take to get where you want to be in the future?
- Exploding the myths that may rise up to trip the older businessperson. How can you squash the very common illusion that people over 50 are sexless, alike, senile, serene, inflexible, uneducatable, unproductive, cranky, difficult and forgetful?
- Tapping your creativity. How can you effectively reach into the storehouse of creativity each of us possesses?
- Mixing a generous dose of enthusiasm with motivation. How do you give yourself that extra push to look self-assuredly toward the future?

• Bringing all the areas of your life into harmony. How do you balance learning, work, family and play in a busy life?

• Volunteering for all the right reasons. How do you find the best opportunities for volunteerism?

• Addressing the unique financial needs of the later years. How do you plan for a life free of money worries?

• Staying in top physical condition. How do you develop a strategy for remaining healthy?

In addition to detailing strategies developed at The Institute for Success Over 50, *Blueprint for Success* lists a number of excellent reference books you can consult during your business explorations. It furnishes a number of checklists and worksheets to help you take inventory of your aptitude for going into business. Further, *Blueprint for Success* goes into great detail on various types of businesses so you can compile a shopping list of those most suited to your experience and expectations. After you have finished this section of the book you will have a better understanding of your place in the entrepreneurial world.

At this point, *Blueprint for Success* takes you step-by-step through the nuts and bolts of developing and organizing your business. Included are guidelines on how to avail yourself of the best tools for your business, strategies for contacting the best people (accountants, insurance agents, lawyers, financiers, bankers, associates, etc.), and methods of tapping information from experts in your field. *Blueprint for Success* familiarizes you with the standard business forms you will come in contact with all through your entrepreneurial exercise. Finally, *Blueprint for Success* introduces you to dozens of people just like yourself—empty-nesters, retired executives, divorced women, investors, husbands and wives looking for a business they can run together, retired military personnel, and factory workers—who wanted to do more with their later years than pull up a rocking chair and tune out. These people tell how they found success in their own businesses.

Joy of a Lifetime

I wrote this book to guide you through what could be one of the greatest adventures of your life—that of starting a new business. Running a business, and running it the right way, is a delight. I have always enjoyed my business ventures to the maximum. After graduating from the University of Illinois in 1939 I went to work for the R. H. Macy Company in New York as a member of its "executive training squad." At night I attended the New York Business School, where I subsequently taught an advertising class.

Later I entered my family's business, Myers Brothers Department Store. I spent the next 40 years there and eventually became its president and C.E.O. The business thrived, grew into a very successful eight-store operation, and enjoyed a reputation as one of the ten highest-quality stores in the United States. Eventually we sold the business to the P. A. Bergner Company, another of America's top retail stores.

At that point, when most other individuals would begin looking for a place to retire, I started a chain of 16 very successful travel agencies. Then I started a coal exporting business, formed a hot-air-balloon company, helped organize a telemarketing catalog business, wrote the bestselling *Success Over Sixty*, and subsequently organized The Institute for Success Over 50 to help other mature Americans enjoy similar accomplishments.

I've had my successes and I've had my failures. I'm also very quick to acknowledge that. I've learned almost as much from failure as I have from success. By sharing all my experiences, I hope to provide you with a shortcut to entrepreneurial success.

The Game of Life

We Americans love games, and one of our favorites is football. I compare football with life: Both are highly competitive, and both require a game plan to be successful.

Like football, life comprises four quarters: The first covers birth through age 25, the second 26 through 50, the third, 51 through 75, and the fourth 76 through 100. And the experiences we have in each quarter directly affect how we play the next.

In *Blueprint for Success* I have you examine what went on in the early quarters of your life because these events will have a great effect on all the decisions you make later—and upon your decision to go into business for yourself. During the first two quarters of life most of us were so busy educating ourselves, advancing our careers and raising our families that we had little time to take stock of who we really were and what we really wanted for our futures.

To fulfill your dream of owning your own business, you must begin by outlining and assessing the life experiences of the first two quarters of your life. As you assess both the personal and professional highlights of each quarter you will begin to see a pattern; a design that shows where your talents, business preferences and successes lie. That is your first clue.

The past holds many clues to what will happen with the rest of your life. The Greek god Janus had two faces: One looked forward into the future, the other looked back into the past. It is very important that those of us who have reached the halfway mark in our lives have *three* faces: one looking at yesterday, one at today and one at tomorrow. By being aware of who you were and who you are, you can start to figure out who you want to be.

Play by Play

During the first quarter of your life you may have developed career skills you never used because of circumstances beyond your control. Your family situation and your upbringing were instrumental in influencing the directions and patterns of the rest of your life. But also during that period you formed skills and interests, you received your formal education, chose your first career, and started your own family. You figured the future would take care of itself.

In the second quarter you settled into your chosen lifestyle and pursued your career. For many of you, this was when you first began taking an introspective look at yourself. Maybe you started a plan. You raised your children, became involved in a community. This was a time when some of you faced divorce, career changes, relocation and/or health problems.

Your experiences during those first two quarters give you all you need to set up a game plan for the third and fourth quarters. The average man will probably live to be 79 years of age and the average woman 84—enough time to go into several businesses, if that is your desire.

Each of you has the potential to live a fuller and happier life than at any previous time in human history. Just as important, each of you has the potential for success beyond your wildest dreams. So read on for some guidelines on how to unleash your imagination, your potential—and your dreams.

IS A SMALL BUSINESS FOR YOU?

Business Facts Almanac

"It's so American to start one's own business."
—Anne McDonnell Ford

This book is in four sections, each preceded by a compendium of tests, worksheets, pertinent quotations and interesting facts designed to get you in the proper frame of mind to better digest the chapters that follow.

PART I comprises five chapters designed to help you assess your situation so you can see if you're really suited and prepared to start a business. This section also offers practical advice for strengthening areas in which you may be weak.

Starting a business, like beginning any endeavor in life, involves taking a risk. Three out of five new businesses fail in the first two years. Yet risk is a natural part of growth and life. More than 60 percent of all new jobs in the United States are generated by new businesses.

"Security is mostly a superstition. It does not exist in nature.
. . . Avoiding danger is no safer in the long run than outright
exposure. Life is either a daring adventure or nothing."
—Helen Keller

1

It is not necessary to be an entrepreneur to be successful in a business. Although having entrepreneurial skills helps, many non-entrepreneurs do well in "turnkey businesses"—those that are already set up so one merely needs to turn the key in the door and go to work.

The most valuable asset of someone over 50 is his or her experience. This will count more than many skills.

> *"Experience is not what happens to a man; it is what man does with what happens to him."*
>
> —Aldous Huxley

Good experiences are just as valuable as those we characterize as bad.

> *"Good people are good because they've come to wisdom through failure."*
>
> —William Saroyan

We learn more from our failures than we do from our successes because there's no ego involved. Experience is the one thing you have plenty of when you are too old to get a job—so why not start your own business?

In the thousands of letters received in response to my book and articles written about me, the most frequently asked question was and still is:

Should I Go Into Business for Myself?

To answer that all-important question, take the following quiz (excerpted from *Success Over Sixty* by C. Andersen and A. Myers [Summit Books, 1984]). Be honest with yourself. Remember, having one's own business is not for everyone.

Answer the following questions, yes or no.

1. Do I have the experience?
2. Have I enough information to organize my own business?
3. Do I have a hobby I can market?
4. Do I have the ability to work and direct people?
5. Do I understand the risks of having my own business?
6. Can I maintain my present standard of living if I start a business of my own?
7. Does the community need my service or product?
8. Will my service or product be needed in the future?
9. Have I determined who my customers will be?
10. Do I know the income level of my customers?
11. Can I estimate the potential growth of my service or product?
12. Have I determined the number and size of my competitors?
13. Is there room in the market for my service or product?
14. Can I capitalize on my competition's weakness?
15. Will technology change my market?
16. Is the market overcrowded with my service or product?
17. Have I researched the successes and failures of similar businesses?
18. Have I protected my idea?
19. Have I a good location?
20. Should I form a proprietorship?
21. Should I buy a franchise?
22. Should I buy a going business?
23. Should I form a partnership?
24. Do I understand the different forms of business?
25. Do I know how to form my type of business?
26. Do I have an attorney who will help me?
27. Do I have an overall promotion plan?
28. Have I a marketable name?
29. Have I considered putting together a small board of experts who can help me?

30. Do I know what media (direct-mail, newspapers, magazines, radio, television) I will use in my advertising?

31. Do I know advertising costs?

32. Do I have an advertising budget?

33. Do I need the help of an agency or advertising person?

34. Have I developed a good logo for my business cards, stationery and advertising?

35. Is my idea protected by copyright or a patent?

36. Can I get local publicity for the business?

37. Do I have enough capital?

38. Do I have enough reserve?

39. Can I survive financially if the business fails?

40. Do I have a realistic growth plan?

41. How much business must I do to make a profit?

42. Have I studied a profit-and-loss statement of a like business?

43. Have I had, or had prepared, a *pro-forma* balance sheet?

44. Do I have sufficient bank connections and borrowing power?

45. Is the payback on my capital realistic?

46. Do I need someone to share my investments?

47. Do I need a bookkeeper or accountant to set up my books?

48. Can I afford to put my company on a computer?

49. Do I have inventory control?

50. Do I plan to prepare a monthly statement?

51. Have I prepared a budget?

52. Do I have expense control in my business?

53. Do I plan to set up a system of credit and collections?

54. Do I have a system for accounts payable?

55. Do I have a system for accounts receivable?

56. Do I have reliable suppliers?

57. Can I keep the costs of materials in line to be competitive and make a profit?

58. Can I establish credit with my suppliers?

59. Can I count on delivery of materials?

60. Can I get discounts by purchasing quantities?

61. Will my suppliers give me extra time to pay?

62. On what terms can I purchase supplies?

63. Do I know my market (who, what, when and where)?

64. Can I operate the business myself?

65. How many employees will I need?

66. Can I manage the lead personnel?

67. Am I capable of training personnel?

68. Do I understand employee health laws, wage-and-hour laws, age laws and unemployment insurance?

69. Do I have an insurance plan for my business and employees?

70. Do I have an accountant or bookkeeper to guide me on employment regulations?

If you answered "yes" to the majority of the above questions, you are ready to go into business for yourself. But your "no" answers are just as important: They indicate the areas where you will have to find answers. And those answers are in the pages ahead.

"Tomorrow is the most important thing in life. It comes to us at midnight very clean. It's perfect when it arrives and it puts itself in our hands. It hopes we've learned something from yesterday."

—John Wayne

CHAPTER 1

Are You an Entrepreneur?

An entrepreneur is a person who organizes and manages a business; a person with considerable initiative who is willing to take risk; a person who has the character and disposition to willingly risk and assume the management of a business.

Not everyone is qualified or has the temperament to organize his or her own business. In fact, you do not have to be an entrepreneur to be successful in business. Many people succeed by entering a turnkey business situation. In other words, they simply turn the key in a door to an already-existing business and start work.

However, having entrepreneurial skills is certainly helpful. Entrepreneurs are convinced they can make their ideas succeed. They believe in their plan so much they can convince others that their ideas will succeed. Harlan Sanders was 72 when he took his mother's recipe, got in his car and traveled the United States until he found enough people to believe in his idea. That idea blossomed as Kentucky Fried Chicken.

Entrepreneurs believe so much in their plans or ideas that they don't even entertain thoughts of failure. They will wait, if necessary, until others come around to their way of thinking. For 35 years Tom Duck worked as an insurance salesman. At the age of 62 he started the Ugly Duckling Rent-A-Car System in Tucson, Arizona. Today, at 75, he is president of an $84.5 million enterprise that is the fifth largest auto-rental firm in the United States.

Entrepreneurs are so convinced that their products or services are better than those currently in the marketplace that they remain unintimidated by what is already out there. They know their ideas have merit and are willing to take on any and all competition. In his 60s, Charles Lubin went to Chicago with an idea for a better quality coffeecake. His daughter was named Sara and his son Lee, and his coffeecake grew into the multi-million-dollar Sara Lee empire.

Elements of an Entrepreneur

Entrepreneurs exhibit certain traits:

1. **The need to achieve.** Entrepreneurs set goals in their lives and seek singular responsibility for their achievements. They see few differences between work and recreation. In fact, they love their work because it is such an integral part of their lives. They are not status-seekers, however. Position or title or the like means little to them. They know that no job—be it emptying the trash, manning the cash-register or watching the door—is beneath them if it helps them reach their goals.

2. **The ability to handle risk.** Entrepreneurs are risk-takers, although they don't necessarily go for the longshots. They take calculated risks and treat any setback as an opportunity for learning. Entrepreneurs know how to manage risk, how to plan contingencies.

Following are just a few of the risks entrepreneurs face:

- Insufficient cash
- Called loan
- Unregistered business name
- Lawsuits
- Theft
- Fire
- Death of a partner
- Investigation by a government agency

- Natural disaster
- Product failure
- Rent increase
- New competition

3. Experience and intelligence. Entrepreneurs stay in their field of experience. They also exhibit a high degree of intelligence and common sense. Most important, they are humble enough to admit they may not know all the answers, bright enough to seek out someone who does.

4. Drive, energy and commitment. Entrepreneurs take care of themselves because they know that if their mental and/or physical health suffers, so do their businesses. They push hard toward their goals, but know their limits.

5. Persistence and common sense. Entrepreneurs cut through obstacles and disappointments with an eye on their goals. They aren't dreamers; they're realists. Entrepreneurs expect difficulty and they stay with a problem until they succeed. They don't drive around endlessly when they become lost; they stop and ask directions.

6. Confidence. Entrepreneurs believe in themselves and their experience. They know they can succeed. They pick their goals carefully and believe in their choices. They don't worry about failing— even if, on occasion, they do.

7. A sense of challenge. Entrepreneurs find completing a challenge the ultimate high. They do not procrastinate, because they view their projects with anticipation and excitement.

8. Creativity. Entrepreneurs relish finding new solutions to old problems. Like artists, they are able to see things in a new and better way.

9. The ability to delegate. Entrepreneurs know when to delegate work and hand over a job to another. They are happy to give employment and encouragement to others. Entrepreneurs know that employees never work whole-heartedly for a boss who feels compelled to do it all.

BELIEVE IN YOUR FUTURE.

Study the foregoing traits. Do you possess all of them? Probably not. Not every entrepreneur does. Study your weak points. Then look for a partner who is strong where you are weak. Many a business has flourished because of a combination of complementary personalities.

What Have I Got to Lose?

One of the advantages of going into business after age 50 is the ability to handle fear. Older entrepreneurs can ask themselves, "What have I got to lose?" and get a different answer than younger businesspersons. After looking at the successes of their first 50 years, examining the equity and experiences they have gained, they can see that they have a much more comfortable margin as to what they can afford to lose.

After such a revelation, many older and first-time entrepreneurs can release themselves from the fear of failure. Putting aside that fear once and for all is putting aside a major obstacle that allows your entrepreneurial skills to shine through.

After you get over the fear of going into business, you have to make sure you're not starting a business with a hidden agenda. Are you going into business to prove something to someone else? Are you trying to show the specter of your father or mother that you're really not lazy and worthless? Are you going ahead in a gesture of defiance to answer someone's nagging?

It is of the utmost importance that you pursue your business ideas because you believe in them, not because you have something to prove to someone. Be truthful with yourself. Look at your motives honestly. Be sure you don't let a longstanding burr under your saddle muddle your thinking or sidetrack your energies.

Another wrong reason for going into business is a need for validation. Are you starting a business because you need or want attention? When you talk to others about your business ideas, are you self-assuredly sharing concepts you sincerely believe in, or are you seeking a boost for your own faltering ego? If the latter, you will do nothing but radiate self-doubt and eventually hamper your business skills.

An inability to accept constructive criticism can also sidetrack your burgeoning entrepreneurial skills. Do you resent criticism? Do you automatically discount harsh words about your business, no matter how well-intentioned? Look at criticism as an opportunity to learn. Advice and criticism are other people's way of telling you what they would do in your situation. Listen. You don't have to follow their advice to the letter. But listen for whatever truth or direction might be there. Criticism should never be taken personally. The minute you become defensive about it you start defending your ideas rather than explaining them. And this attitude will cloud your feelings and choke your entrepreneurial thinking.

Finally, the most undesirable of all traits to watch out for is— laziness. There is no faster way to kill an entrepreneurial spirit than to drown it in procrastination. Often the only way an idea can succeed is to be carried out immediately.

As you go down this list of negative traits, remember that you're not perfect. But if you feel you have any of these problems, be aware of them and work to eradicate them. Remember, having all positive traits and no negative ones is not an automatic guarantee of success. You must possess managerial skills to get your project off the ground. You must also use the proper network to obtain information and weave a safety-net of experts to help you carry out your new endeavor.

Now that you know the positive and negative traits of an entrepreneur, go on to the next chapters of this book; they identify the skills that sustain the entrepreneurial spirit and ensure ultimate business success.

CHAPTER 2

Your Secret Weapons

Your secret weapons in the fight to establish a successful business are the skills, ideas and talents you have developed over the past 50-plus years. Those experiences give you unique insights into the workings of the world around you that most younger people have yet to develop. By carefully assessing these assets you can gain not only a sense of pride and security in your abilities, but also an excellent weapon to help you zero in on your business target.

The Boomers Are Coming!

As the 21st century approaches, a very interesting phenomenon is about to occur. The first of the Baby Boomers are about to enter their 50s. Their dominance in the population has affected America every decade since they were born: In the '50s they made us all family-oriented; in the '60s they made us hip to protest and change; in the '70s and '80s they became the ultimate consumers. And you can be assured they will leave their own unique imprint on aging in America as they enter their second half-century.

Once it was believed that if you could start a business or fad that appealed to the Baby Boomers you would make millions. Thus the successes of pet rocks, hula hoops and the like. As the Boomers grew older, fast foods, T-shirts and personal computers with messages became the sales successes. Your age and experience give you

USE YOUR SECRET WEAPONS.

an advance clue as to what the Boomers will "need" in the coming decades. Use this intuition wisely.

Keep this in mind when you listen to Paul Hawken's first piece of advice on his public television series, *Growing a Business*. "Start as a customer. . . . Business opportunities are more than ample today for the simple reason that many American consumers are dissatisfied. My business started from being a customer who did not like what I bought. I suspect your business will begin that way too. You know what you want to replace, improve or change. So begin where the tool breaks, the service slips or the shoe pinches." Hawken is the co-founder of Smith & Hawken, a very successful mail-order garden-supply company that blossomed from his dissatisfaction with garden tools that self-destructed after just a few months' use.

Examples of entrepreneurs who built successful businesses because of their dissatisfaction with certain products abound:

Many years ago, Klaus Obermeyer went to Aspen, Colorado, to ski. He was always getting too cold or too warm on the slopes. Clothes available for the sport were too cumbersome. Nothing on the market provided him with lightweight, warm and versatile fashions for skiing—so he started a sportswear company that marketed just that. It is now one of the world's most successful firms.

Phil B. worked all his life as regional manager for a muffler company. He had great contacts and many chances to visit successful garages. When his company decided to replace him with a younger man, Phil didn't go—he got going. Instead of opting for retirement he joined two friends in putting together and starting a superior garage service. Today their business flourishes.

The Writers Co-Op of Santa Fe, New Mexico, was born as a result of a business crisis in the publishing industry. The founders of the Co-Op observed that more and more books were being marketed to readers in New York, Chicago and Los Angeles, with less and less emphasis on distribution to the rest of the country. Stan Steiner, president of the Writers Co-Op, observed that "there are 225 million people outside of the New York, Chicago and Los Angeles areas

who read books. How do you get books to them when Eastern publishers don't even try?'' They enlarged and changed some of the
marketing strategies of the New York publishers—and created a
highly successful marketing network that reaches the smaller markets of New Mexico, Arizona and southern Colorado. Business is
more than very good. It is excellent.

Chuck Loomis spent 30 years as a sales manager for Pacific Bell
of California. After he retired he researched various business possibilities and decided that one major growth industry that would
utilize his experience was car phones. During his first year selling
the phones he generated $250,000 in sales. He now has seven full-
time employees and is going full tilt. Loomis, who packaged a combination of his skills from a past career and current savvy, points
out that as an older entrepreneur he was able to more quickly
establish a line of credit—an essential for any starting business.

Look carefully at the above examples and blend their various
strengths with the fact that you're over 50, with all the experience
that entails, and you'll find yourself sitting in the catbird seat when
it comes to a formula for starting a successful business. You've been
there and you've seen it many times. The realization that most of
America will soon be your age is a definite plus. Use your first-hand
knowledge of what older customers want to build a business.

Other Weapons of the Trade

Other skills mastered over a lifetime—being able to please people,
make people smile, recruit people to your point of view—will ultimately help you build a clientele for your new business. Your memories, experiences, insights and patience, fine-tuned through the
years, are equally valuable assets.

Some of the finer points of business relationships and successes
evolve directly from attributes acquired and developed over a lifetime. In too many cases they have, for whatever reason, gone out

BRING BACK THE
GOOD OLD STANDARDS OF THE PAST.

of style. You will do well to revive them as you work to set up a new business:

1. Establish high standards. You have the advantage of remembering when quality and fine service were the rule instead of the exception. Use these to your advantage.

2. Practice old-fashioned courtesy. Your generation was well versed in the finer points of etiquette and gracious manners. Use this ability to get the best from your employees and give the best to your customers.

3. Rely on intuition. It takes years to develop intuition. You are in a position now to call on that well-developed sense.

4. Remain serene. Maturity tends to help an individual keep things in perspective. Let the calmness and patience that come naturally in later life sustain you through the storm of starting a new business. You know better than anyone at this point that storms do pass.

5. Share information. The ability to communicate is probably at your command since your education stressed the three R's. Use your skills to make your desires understood whether you are talking to a financier or to an employee. Sharing information makes a business work.

Older people sharing and drawing upon their decades of experience is a definite wave of the future in the business world. *Years are the ultimate "trade secret"* for the legions of us entering the second half of life.

Taking Proper Aim

It is important to keep in mind that even the most powerful secret weapon will be ineffective if it is not aimed properly. To bring your target into the crosshairs you must take inventory of your skills before undertaking a new business. By assessing your education, career and personal experiences you can zero in on the business that will result in the greatest success for you.

One of my friends always enjoyed art during her school years. Her talent was recognized in high school when she won a poster contest. But she put her skill on the shelf for the next 50 years while she pursued a career in law (at her family's urging). After she retired from a successful career with a prestigious law firm, she went back to art and established a small but very successful greeting-card and stationery company that caters to resort boutiques. This business allowed her to bring a skill out of the attic, brush it off and put it to work. So don't forget those unused, all but forgotten abilities. They may be a key to your business success.

Combining innate talents with acquired skills to come up with your own formula for a new business is very important. Mary M. worked for years as a word processor. During those years she developed a skill for designing and producing pamphlets, brochures and other types of advertising. When desktop-publishing software came on the market, she took aim at starting a business of her own. "I began practicing with my program to see how fast I could complete a job. I estimated how long each one would take and priced my work accordingly. At first I took longer than estimated to complete jobs, but I did not pass those charges on to the customer. Now I can whip out a job faster than I ever expected." Her home-based business is highly lucrative. Sometimes, during peak periods, she even has to hire temporary help.

If some of those mothballed abilities need freshening, take the steps necessary to do just that. A homemaker I know took her early talent in mathematics and her years of balancing the family checkbook and budget to school. She attended adult-education classes in bookkeeping, earned a degree, and eventually parlayed her experiences into a career as a C.P.A. She started out working from her home with a few clients. Today she has her own firm with three full-time employees.

A Personal Inventory

If someone asked you to submit an autobiographical sketch that included your background, history, present situation, and long- and short-range plans, could you do it? If not, answer the following questions. They will help you identify your skills and give you direction:

1. Do I have a current inventory of my experiences and background?
2. What would I ultimately like to do in business?
3. Who are my most valuable contacts?
4. Do I keep in touch with old acquaintances?
5. Have I made new friends and contacts in the last year?
6. What are the things I value most in life?
7. What are my major interests?
8. What do I see as my future lifestyle?
9. What are my present financial needs?
10. What are my future financial goals and plans?
11. Do I have alternative business plans?
12. Do I have alternative personal plans?
13. What special skills and qualifications do I have?
14. What are my most important business achievements?
15. What are my most important personal achievements?
16. What are my immediate objectives?
17. Am I prepared to learn new skills?
18. Do I read magazines, books and newspapers to broaden my vision and keep my thinking contemporary?
19. Do I have a lifelong-learning plan?
20. Do I attend and absorb lectures? Night-school classes? Seminars? Do I watch public service programs on radio and TV?
21. Do I want to develop new hobbies and learn new sports?
22. What are my long-range objectives?
23. What are my short-range objectives?
24. How long do I want to stay where I am?
25. How well do I manage my time?

CHAPTER 3

The Six Transferable Attributes

Up to now this book has described basic business principles, given you several checklists, and warned you of business pitfalls—all essential when laying the groundwork for your business endeavor. But even more important is your own realization that you have within yourself the skills and potential to organize and run a successful business. Without such a knowledge, all the rest is worth nothing.

Following are six attributes you have that will ultimately help you realize just how business-ready you are:

Attribute 1: The Ability to Cope with Change

More than 20 years ago Alvin Tofler wrote one of the most important books of this century in which he described the acceleration of change in our time. In *Future Shock* he pointed out that there are more than 800 segments of approximately 62 years each in human history. The overwhelming majority of the items we use today were developed in the 800th segment—the years in which you and I are living. You have come of age in this most technologically productive segment in all history. Think of how that has affected you.

Add the rising human longevity rates, which seem to increase each year as medical technology forges ahead. Dirk Pearson and Sandy Shaw suggest the possibility of lifespans of 150 to 200 years within the foreseeable future. Heady stuff, indeed. So resist the inclination to put your lifetime of skills on a shelf when you reach your 50s and 60s and realize that those skills are your primary tools for making the coming years among the most exciting and productive of your life!

You may be holding down a job that is boring or that you hate; your company may be ready to merge, putting your job on the line; you may be on the list for early retirement; you may have just gone through a divorce; you may have just sent off the last of your children; or you may have just lost a spouse. These are all personal alterations that can have a great effect on your life, but only you can determine whether the result will be positive or otherwise.

The ability to handle change from within *and* without, as well as to keep up with world developments and trends: These are key skills when starting a new business. Look around you. The really successful businesses never sit still, never rest on their laurels. They are always changing, trying out new ideas and discarding some, retaining others. Keeping a business successful is more than just worrying about sales and profits.

In every field those who recognize and embrace change are the ones who succeed. The Nordstrom chain of department stores was built on the observation that people want service; this at a time when most other major concerns were riding high on the self-serve wave. Most recently, thousands of companies have jumped on the environmental bandwagon with products and services that cater to the world's realization that we have to preserve what is left of Mother Earth.

So know you have what it takes to capitalize on all kinds of changes, including those within you. In your 50 or more years you have gone through numerous transitions: where you live, your profession, attitudes, hobbies, what you read and listen to, what you eat and drink. All these restructurings affect the type of entrepreneurial endeavor you choose.

Take the case of Bill Barnaby. Barnaby was a dental technician with his own lab most of his 60 years. But he always took great pride in a much-loved hobby: Chinese antiques. Every weekend he would scour shops and sales near and far in search of these treasures. As time went on he became an expert in appraising jade, cloisonné, cinnabar and the like. Then one day he decided it was time to take a new business path. He sold his lab, opened his own antique shop, and has become successful beyond his most optimistic expectations. All because he knew when the time was right.

Change is all around us all the time. Go to a supermarket and really look at what people are eating these days: Low-cholesterol, low-sodium, low-fat foods; decaffeinated coffees and herb teas; microwave meals and snacks—all answers to changes in attitudes and needs that have come about in the last couple of decades. Attend an electronics show or visit an electronics store. All of those now-common items—answering machines, computers, VCRs, cellular telephones, fax machines and the like—have come into vogue within the past ten years or less.

Draw from the changes in *your* life and expand them into the ability to recognize opportunities that are everywhere. Going from micro-experience to macro-experience is a giant step toward finding your business niche.

Attribute 2: An Inquisitive Mind

The second essential skill for the entrepreneur is an inquisitive mind. This involves the desire to research and learn more about things around you today to prepare for tomorrow.

The brain is like a muscle. If it's not exercised, it atrophies. The wisdom gained through half a century of experience has brought you to the realization that a sedentary life physically *or* mentally is a deadly life. So now is the time to organize your time so you can pursue activities that will keep you fit both ways. Enroll in adult education or college classes, attend seminars, join an exercise group, ride a stationary bike, attend expositions and shows on business development and franchising. Allow your imagination to run wild. Allow yourself to dream.

Alex Comfort points out in his book, *A Good Age*, that the acquisition of both new skills and additional education are natural parts of the second half of life. Contrary to one shopworn stereotype, there is no lessening of the ability of healthy people to assimilate new ideas and skills as they age. If anything, because they're building on an already rich foundation of knowledge, they often find learning easier than their younger counterparts.

A 70-year-old who had worked all his adult life as a laborer showed up at a seminar filled with Harvard graduates, professors and eminent scholars. When each attendee was asked why he or she was taking the course, this one said simply, "I want to die an educated man."

Jean R. spent most of her life working as a private secretary. At the age of 65 she moved to California and began looking for work. She had a number of interviews with no luck. Realizing she would have to take a different track, she enrolled in a local college to learn how to operate a computer. She hoped to eventually start a computer typing service from her home.

It wasn't easy. During her first class when the instructor asked if anyone was intimidated by the computer, Jean was the only one to raise her hand; but in the end she was among the top students. Later she purchased her own computer, laser printer, copy and fax machines and went into business. Soon she had all the clients she could handle. An added twist: Jean now *teaches* the class in which she initially held up her hand!

Len B.'s career was in real estate and construction—until he bought his movie camera. He became obsessed with it and enrolled in a top California film school taking courses in such various aspects of filmmaking as writing, editing, producing and directing. Later he risked some capital to produce educational and children's films. His

The Velveteen Rabbit sold big in both U.S. and foreign markets. Then he produced a film about the senior market; and his prize-winning documentary, *Women in Business,* was used by the Small Business Administration all across the country. Len proved conclusively that a mature person can not only learn new skills but excel.

So sort out, organize, and utilize the knowledge you've acquired. Build on areas of interest. And dare to try, again.

Attribute 3: Connecting

Networking is the dynamic process whereby we make connections with others who share our interests, skills and ideals. In Jules Willing's book, *The Lively Mind,* he aptly described the impetus for networking:

> "For me the acme of lively mindedness, of creativity, is the connection with others—the reaching out and touching—the sending of the message and receiving of the response—the act of joining and evolving. It is this contact, the joy of this engagement . . . that is self-enlarging and self-energizing, that evokes vigor and replenishes joy."

One of the great advertising campaigns of the '80s was AT&T's "Reach Out and Touch Someone." The company encouraged us to call family, friends and business contacts to renew and sustain friendships, share information and make connections. During a research project at MIT Michael Guerenten asked a varied group of individuals to keep lists of all the people they would normally come in contact with during a 100-day period. On the average, each listed about 500 names.

Social psychologist Stanley Melgram, who conducted a number of experiments with networking, finds that Americans generally have a pool of 500 to 2,500 acquaintances.

When you have lived 50 years or more, you have compiled a virtual encyclopaedia of people, organizations and places. From this rich resource you can pull a list of people who will willingly help you start your own business.

In my own lifetime I have built, nourished and retained a human network that comprises people in almost every line of business including politics, finance, travel, real estate, franchising, merchandising and importing. I know accountants, physicians, writers, religious leaders, philanthropists, publishers, homemakers, diplomats, educators and attorneys.

Every time I organize a new business I dip into this great pool and gain invaluable advice and information that can't be found in any book. In essence, I collect people. I encourage you to do the same.

And I never hesitate to contact an acquaintance, no matter how long ago I knew him or her. Some years ago, when I was starting a coal business, I needed some information on how coal was used by the cement industry. I remembered that in high school I played football with Tom Sheets, who became the West Coast president of Portland Cement. I called him. He didn't know who I was until I reminded him that I was the guard who played next to him some 50 years earlier. He was delighted to hear from me and gladly gave me the information I needed.

One of the biggest failings in networking is disorganization. Certainly you cannot keep a half century of information in your head. For years, I kept an address book that served me well. Eventually my network grew so large that the only way I could contain it was in a computer. I can truthfully say my network has been one of the largest single contributing factors to my many business successes over the years.

Here are ten basic tips for organizing and maintaining a network that have worked well for me:

1. **Organize.** Devise a method of keeping track of and storing

network information. You don't need to go into painful detail about the individuals; just list each person's name, company, phone number and area of expertise.

2. Share your network. Be willing to give networking information to others. Remember, what goes around comes around—and that is doubly true when it comes to business courtesy.

3. Network in your community. Take full advantage of local networking opportunities: fraternal bodies, your place of worship, historical societies, alumni associations, museum auxiliaries, service clubs, hospital volunteer groups and the like. If you give time to your community through such organizations you will come to work with countless people who can be reliable contacts for years to come.

4. Take the time to pay compliments. If you read a book or magazine article you find really valuable, write a note of appreciation. If some organization performs a service that affects you in a positive way, do the same. One of the sweetest phrases in the English language is thank you.

5. Connect whenever possible. Talk to people. Develop a genuine interest in your fellow beings. When you're around people —talk to them. Find out where a person is from, volunteer information about a special restaurant or a good show a vacationer might be interested in, share a story with a stranger. Most people are happy to take part in conversation; they just have to be approached in the right way.

6. Keep in touch. Don't let people slip away. Too often we make friends and then lose them because one of us moves or changes jobs. We may think they aren't interested in keeping in touch. But when you show enough interest in people to maintain contact with them, your action is rarely ignored and almost always appreciated.

7. Share your time and expertise willingly. Give as much of yourself as you hope your network contacts will give you. One of the greatest satisfactions in life is knowing that you really had a positive effect on another person's life. Never become too busy or too isolated to help others.

8. Listen. This is the one most neglected skill in our culture. If you don't know how to really listen, learn. If you are a good listener you will gain much more than knowledge—you will gain the undying respect of everyone you know.

9. Ask questions. Make your queries friendly and intelligent, then refer back to step 8. Be genuinely interested in people and you will ultimately uncover whole worlds of information that will be useful to you in all areas of your life.

10. Save your judgment for another day. Take the attitude that you can make even the most introverted and unfriendly individual a friend and ally. Don't let another's negative opinions about someone sway you. Meeting people is not about popularity. It is about experiencing humanity in all its varied forms.

Attribute 4: Self-Reliance

Self-reliance takes a lifetime to develop. We are born completely dependent. We go through school systems that do little to break that dependence. Then, one day, we're expected to go off and live our own lives *on* our own. Over the years we develop other dependencies—on people, on places, on jobs, etc. But eventually we have to learn that the only people we can really depend on are ourselves. Once you get used to this idea, you will come to relish your independence and fight anyone who tries to take it from you.

Often the realization that you are the only one you can depend on comes about during a crisis: job loss, divorce, death of a spouse, forced retirement, relocation. Yet though self-realization is often hard-learned, I've never heard anyone complain about his or her new-found independence once it's been achieved.

You must be able to recognize the negative times as opportunities for positive learning and change, however. The Chinese symbol for "crisis" translates loosely as "dangerous opportunity." In the midst of a crisis we tend to become mired in its negative aspects and it seems easier to just retreat and give up. But if you keep in mind that almost every crisis is an opportunity for positive change, you will not only shorten a painful period, you will be more receptive to positive avenues of action that open up then.

If you hadn't lost your job, been divorced or widowed, had to retire or relocate, you might never have thought about starting your own business. Remember: Each of us has the ability and skill to not only overcome crisis and change, but to use the lessons learned during trying times as a foundation on which to build a new life.

Model Kaylan Pickford forged a successful career from a highly traumatic divorce, remarriage and the agony of watching her second husband die of cancer. Devastated, she withdrew from life and wallowed in her sorrows. But finally she realized that if she didn't do something, and quickly, she would lose everything—her self-esteem, her health and her independence. Knowing she must get back out in the world, she moved to New York and enrolled in an acting school with an eye toward eventually working in commercials. Then, as a middle-aged woman at a time when Madison Avenue considered a model over the hill at 25, she took on the advertising industry.

She asked the wary admen logical questions: Didn't older women drive automobiles, use cosmetics, wear clothes, etc.? Did a woman stop being a consumer when she turned 40? The answers were inescapable—and Pickford became the leader of a whole cadre of mature female models. She later wrote in her book, *Always a Woman*, that "Everyone has a role in life. No one else should tell you what yours is. Though it may be hard work, it needs to be discovered and identified."

All this doesn't mean you should wait for a crisis to change your life so you can achieve the success you really want. It *does* mean that you are the only one who can make your dream of starting a business reality. Only you can reach for every iota of independence and self-reliance and move forward with your dream.

Attribute 5: Talent

We are all born with innate capacities that set us apart from others. The saddest waste is an undiscovered (or worse, ignored) talent. Now is the time to take stock of your aptitudes, develop them, and use them as a basis for your new business.

A friend of mine had been a lathe operator all his working life. Three years before he was due to retire, he discovered his pension would not be enough to live comfortably after retirement. But instead of panicking, he started planning. He canvassed the area where he lived and found there was only one machine shop, and it was doing very well. He began converting a garage into a shop. He took a course on developing a business, started purchasing equipment and doing small jobs in his fledgling shop. By the time he did retire, he was able to segue smoothly into his own business.

Today this man makes much more money than he did at his original job. And, with the help of his son, he can travel and play golf whenever he wants. This is a classic example of how one person planned ahead, tapped his skills, and relied on his own expertise to develop a very successful business.

George L. is another example. He worked in the garden department of a major retail chain for many years. Then he took the knowledge gained in that job and built on it. He began taking classes in landscaping; on his days off he worked with a friend who was a landscaper; he even squeezed in visits to plant wholesalers when he went on vacation. While traveling, he began to notice how many big office buildings and restaurants were filled with plants. He asked around and found out they were provided by rental companies.

When he found there were no plant-rental companies in his area, he made up a brochure, distributed it widely, and eventually drummed up enough business to begin working part-time as a supplier of rental plants. He kept his job for a while, but when his own business became sufficiently successful he took early retirement. By initiating a transition period, George was able to test his entrepreneurial idea while still secure in his paid job. It took a lot of work, but in the long run his extra efforts paid off handsomely.

Now is the time to make an inventory of all the skills and talents you have. Study the list carefully and see which ones could be developed into a business. Make step-by-step plans that will slowly and methodically lead you from your present situation into one where you own and run your own business. Then get going!

Attribute 6: Commitment

We've identified five of the six attributes that will be most helpful in laying the groundwork for your new business. Now you will be able to view change as an opportunity; inquire about ways to polish your business acumen; develop a network of people to help you; build on your self-reliance; and polish and expand on already existing talents to apply to your business.

None of this will be worth anything, however, unless you have the fifth attribute: commitment. That shouldn't be too hard. Committing isn't new to you. You've been doing it all your life. You initially made a commitment to your mother and father, to your teachers, to an employer, to your spouse and children, and to your creditors, to name a few. Every day when you get up, you commit yourself to doing the best you can with what you have.

Let's go through some of the prerequisites of developing a new business. First you must have a firm commitment based on clearly defined objectives. Therefore, you need to inventory your reasons for becoming an entrepreneur. List—*in writing*—every motive:

DO YOUR HOMEWORK—BUILD THE FOUNDATION FIRST!

money, challenge, a better lifestyle, independence, a desire to contribute to society, prestige, etc. Constantly reminding yourself of your goals, whatever they may be, will help you overcome some of the initial trepidation when you actually begin your business.

One good exercise to help you identify your objectives and establish a commitment to them is to write an autobiography. Take the time to outline all of your life accomplishments to date. This will show you in black and white where your strengths are and where your ability to commit carried you to success. Careful study will most likely point out that your greatest victories involved the following.

1. Preparation. Detailed planning is absolutely essential to the success of any business. If you do your spadework carefully and with an honest and pragmatic eye toward the future, you will be ready for any contingency. There is no such thing as too much preparation.

2. Positive thinking. In Norman Vincent Peale's landmark *The Power of Positive Thinking*, he demonstrated that people can do the impossible just by believing they can. This "can-do" attitude is a primary necessity.

3. A desire for success. If you look back over your most rousing successes, you will undoubtedly find that almost without exception you succeeded because you had a passionate desire to do so. A real desire to bring self-satisfaction, enjoyment and a sense of achievement will propel and inspire you to succeed.

4. Belief in yourself. You have developed a certain amount of confidence during your life. Seize and use it as a cornerstone for your entrepreneurial commitment. If you really believe you can do it, chances are you will.

5. A strong work ethic. You can't be afraid of work. Starting any new business involves long working hours and personal sacrifice—but these can be exhilarating experiences too.

6. A blueprint for success. Just as every skyscraper starts with a sheaf of blueprints, the success of your business depends on a detailed design for action. You have all the tools you need; now you must determine when and how to use them. If you look back over your past endeavors, you will see that the most successful were the most meticulously planned.

Commitment is a pledge of allegiance to your goals, to your business plans, and, most important, to yourself. Once you have listed them and have put to paper a workable course of action within the framework of your capabilities, you will have everything in place to succeed. Now all that's left is to follow through!

CHAPTER 4

Use Your Creativity

Most of us don't begin to realize just how creative we are. Many have worked for years at jobs that involved budgeting or intricate business plans; have kept a household going; have sold products; have raised children; have worked diligently with charities; etc. All these involved coming up with new ideas and fresh approaches, yet because they also involve a certain amount of routine, we overlook the creativity they entail.

It is hard for most of us to realize that we have the potential to make our dreams come true and devise marketable products or services that can launch us into business. Bud Grossman, founder of the Minnesota-based multimillion-dollar Gelco Corporation, says automation is becoming creativity's number-one enemy. "The new office technology is a step backwards. The worker gets bored as hell with what he is doing. It may have been hard work, but a person used to sit down and type a letter and identify with it. Now he puts it into one damn machine, changes a few words and produces 1,000 different letters. We have dehumanized the worker."

Grossman has launched an aggressive program within his company to tap the creativity of his managers. "Even if a guy risks and flops," says Grossman, "he learns a lot. He gains certain confidence from the company because it backs him up. We have to be damn sure we don't scare anybody so much that he will be afraid to float a suggestion or try something different. Ideas are really all we have."

Too often people believe that dreaming of new ideas and products is the exclusive realm of young people. In reality, creativity has nothing to do with a stage of life. The spark lies within every one of us. We need no more than a change in philosophy to make our full inventive powers bloom.

"It's never too late," says Robert Butler, a psychiatrist well known for his studies of creativity in older people. Some of the most imaginative people in human history didn't reach their full potential until their later years: Sophocles, Michelangelo, Titian, Tintoretto, Cervantes, Hals, Haydn, Verdi, Tolstoy, Shaw, Freud, Grandma Moses, Churchhill, Picasso, Hammer, Forbes.

If you can dream, and if you can observe, you can create. First, understand that there are many degrees of inventiveness. The product you conceive for a business may not be as great a creative feat as Tolstoy's *Resurrection*, written when he was 71, but your product will serve its purpose.

George Bernard Shaw wrote in *Back to Methuselah*, "You see things; and you say, 'Why?' But I dream things that never were; and I say, 'Why not?'" This inspiring philosophy applies, at any age, to our capacity to dream and to create.

Look, See, Create

"It is commonly held that there is such a thing as the creative spark," wrote Douglas R. Hofstadter in an article in *Scientific American*. "When a brilliant mind comes up with a new idea or work of art there has been a quantum leap from ordinary mortals. People such as Mozart are held to be divinely inspired, to have magical insights. . . . I contend that the 'creative spark' is not the exclusive property of a few rare individuals, but rather part of the everyday mental activity of everyone, even the most ordinary people."

Wise men and scientists have attempted to quantify the creative process throughout history. One thing they have found is that the human mind follows the line of least resistance; i.e., it is most likely to be creative when at rest. As Hofstadter put it, "The bottom line is that invention is much more like falling off a log than like sawing one in two." Einstein didn't go around racking his brain muttering to himself, "How can I come up with a good idea?" Mozart said, "Things should flow like oil."

Case in point: One day years ago a man was waiting for a bus to take him to his office. He reached into his pocket to pull out some coins to jingle in his hand. He felt a bit of wire, pulled that out instead, and passed the time bending the wire into different shapes. When the bus arrived the man shoved the bent wire back into his pocket. Arriving at work he found his desk, as usual, stacked with correspondence. He began to sort the letters into separate piles and at one point needed something to hold several pieces of mail together. He thought of the piece of wire in his pocket, pulled it out—and invented the paper clip. This man's idle time combined with his powers of observation served him well.

Each of you has the ability to create a new service or product. George Demestral, in his 60s, was pulling burrs from the coats of his hunting dogs after a long hike. As he sat there he began to absentmindedly stick the burrs together and pull them apart. He expanded on the idea until it became what is known today as Velcro. Dupont bought the idea and Demestral made millions from the subsequent royalties.

Joe Segal was a born entrepreneur. He started his first business while in school. He bought a small printing press and sold calling cards to his chums for five cents a hundred. At 15 he started a mail-order business, a little catalog selling advertising specialties to magicians. In June 1964, Segal saw an article in *Time* magazine about the last pure-silver dollars being sold by the U.S. government. A picture accompanying the article showed people lined up around the block waiting to buy silver dollars from the U.S. Treasury in Washington, D.C. That gave Segal his idea—to issue a series of sterling-silver medals, a little larger than silver dollars, and of the highest quality. He hired Gilroy Roberts, chief sculptor at the U.S. Mint, to produce the designs. Thus the Franklin Mint came into being. It took a tremendous amount of work, but within only eight years the business had $100 million in revenues. Today the Franklin Mint deals in dozens of collectors items—books, porcelains, crystal, etc. And it began with an idea gleaned from a magazine article.

Fortune magazine, in a lead article published in February 1990, pegged the '90s as the decade of environmentalism on a global scale. Indeed, people are becoming increasingly dedicated to saving Earth's quickly disappearing resources. Conserving energy and soil, saving forests, preserving the ozone layer and recycling have become almost sacred duties. And there will be an ever-increasing number of products and businesses dedicated to these ends. Home water-purification systems, energy-saving light bulbs, fuel-conserving products and solar energy have all become almost overnight successes. Waste management is quickly becoming another area ripe for entrepreneurial creativity. Anyone starting a new business in this decade would be well advised to take his or her cues from the overwhelming needs in the area of conservation.

Victor Lowe heard the cry of environmentalists who bemoaned the damaging effects of petroleum-based styrofoam packaging. He saw that corporate entities would be receptive to environmentally safe products, if they could be manufactured at a reasonable cost. Lowe was still flush from the success of his dashboard protector that shielded the inside of cars from the hot rays of the sun. So he let his creative powers loose on this packaging dilemma and came up with the idea of pressed popcorn forms to replace the styrofoam kernels used to protect breakables. He calls his company Pop-Pack, Inc., "The All-American, biodegradable, renewable, do-it-yourself answer to industry packaging needs." His is a perfect example of a creative idea that meets the needs of a changing world.

Making things that last longer, go further, work more simply and save more time and energy is a natural for people over 50.

You've had years of experience doing just that. Harnessing that ability and making it work for you through product development and marketing may be the key to your fortune.

Sylvan Goldman ran a small chain of grocery stores in Oklahoma City. One day he was watching a customer struggle with groceries she was trying to balance in a too-full basket she carried in her arms. Turning back to his desk his glance fell on a folding chair in the corner of his office. Something clicked: He saw that he could combine the properties of a folding chair and a basket—and the first shopping cart was developed. Goldman secured a patent and began to manufacture the shopping carts. At first shoppers resisted using the funny-looking vehicles, so Goldman hired people to go into the stores and use them. The idea caught on and within ten years he built the largest shopping-cart business in the world. Then, using the same concept, he invented the portable luggage carrier.

There are hundreds of similar examples. One day Gary Dahl sat casually fingering a smooth stone. Suddenly he realized what a soothing effect this had on him. He described his action as petting the rock, much like stroking a dog—so he called the stone a "Pet Rock." He realized that marketing is the key to the success of any product, so he creatively packaged the idea and sent it to stores all over the country. He made millions of dollars from this one silly idea.

Similarly, Bertha Lackman, a 90-year-old grandmother, had a problem getting her grandchildren to take their baths. To entice them into the bathtub she sewed a wash cloth into the form of a puppet and called it "Scrubb Puppy." It was such a hit with her grandchildren she decided to market it. The product went into major department stores across the country and made her a fortune.

We never know when the spark of creativity will ignite. One day researcher James Schlatter, who was employed by a major pharmaceutical company, was working on the formula for a new medicine. He was mixing a powder and scanning a reference book at the same time. When he put his finger, which had some of the powder on it, to his tongue to moisten it so he could turn the page of the book, he was shocked at the overwhelming sweetness. He had developed NutraSweet.

Creativity in Tandem

Sometimes all that's needed to fire the creative part of your mind is another's creativity. The two minds work in a symbiotic process to create ideas that neither could have come up with alone. An excellent example is the creative relationship between Lawrence Morehouse, former professor of kinesiology at the University of California at Los Angeles. Morehouse, who was in his 60s at the time, worked with other health-minded people to invent the heart-rate controlled bicycle. He wrote the bestselling *Total Fitness*, which introduced new ideas and theories now being used all over the country. In fact, he was instrumental in fueling the craze that made fitness a major U.S. industry.

Morehouse was always combining his ideas with others' to generate useful products. For example, when he was studying the effect of shoe soles on foot function with Nathan Hack, he came up with the ripple sole—which became a major factor in the development of the athletic shoe industry. Other products he was involved with: seats to help pilots withstand the forces of gravity during space flights, ergonomically correct tractor seats for John Deere, and a chair specifically designed for computer operators.

I took an idea about a portable fitness-testing unit to Morehouse. We came up with an exercise program and testing equipment that included a pulse, blood-pressure and breathing monitor combined with a hand-grip strength evaluator and weight-lifting system; all of this fits in an executive briefcase.

Quizzing Your Creativity

Imagination is the key to creativity. In *Success Over Sixty*, co-author Christopher Andersen and I devised a quiz to test your hidden talents and abilities to think creatively:

True or False:

1. I spend too much time daydreaming when I should be working.

2. Prime-time television bores me. I only watch the news.

3. There is no substitute for hard work.

4. There is no such thing as a new idea.

5. I don't have time to read.

6. I never write a letter when I can pick up the phone.

7. No news is good news.

8. Nobody really wants to hear what I think.

9. Curiosity killed the cat.

10. If I haven't set the world on fire by now, I never will.

If you answered true to any of the above, you are probably sabotaging your creative impulses. Here's why:

1. Daydreaming? Don't apologize for letting your mind wander. That is when the fresh idea, the new angle is most likely to strike.

2. TV bores you? The late renowned psychologist B. F. Skinner attributed much of his mental agility in his 70s to "relaxing" the brain with regular doses of prime-time pap and even soaps—the 1990s equivalent of gazing into the hearth. The mind cannot work full steam without fatigue; you need to let your mind go blank sometimes. A study shows that watching TV takes less energy, thought and coordination than eating a meal. How much more relaxed can you get?

3. Oh, yes, there is a substitute for hard work—inspiration. And yes, as we have noted, that usually comes when we are not sweating at all.

4. You think there are no new ideas? What is significant here is the defeatist attitude: You're less likely to open your mind to something new if you've convinced yourself that it's an impossibility. Remember, creativity is often simply taking something already in existence and employing it in a new way.

5. Make time to read. TV news skims the surface, but reading material expands and gives depth to the ideas, plans and events of the world. From this fertile territory are born many creative businesses.

6. You may prefer the phone, but letter-writing is an effective way of clarifying your thoughts and an opportunity to think creatively. Putting your thoughts down on paper distances you from them, allowing you to look at them with new insight.

7. The "no news is good news" philosophy implies a resistance to change, to new ideas. You're not apt to be very creative if you want your world to remain as is.

8. "Nobody wants to hear what I think" is one of those self-defeating (and self-pitying) philosophies that undermine our will to succeed. We are often afraid of looking stupid, of being wrong. But while a bad idea is usually quickly forgotten, a good one can lift you far above the crowd. At any age, it's important to risk a bad idea in the hope of coming up with a good one. Finally, if you've developed this low opinion of yourself because the people around you take you for granted, find a new audience.

9. Curiosity killed the cat? "What if . . . " is part and parcel of a creative person's working vocabulary. A *lack* of curiosity kills creativity!

10. The "if-you-haven't-set-the-world-on-fire-by-now-you-never-will" blues; another instance of defeatism that tramples creative fires.

The Intelligence Myth

Recent studies show that the myth "You can't teach an old dog new tricks" is just that—a myth. "In some areas," according to Harry Moody of New York's Brookdale Center on Aging at Hunter College, "as in tests measuring insight into problem situations, in creative understanding and metaphoric processing, older people show actual statistical *gains*." But the negative self-image ascribed to older people can send them into a spiral of depression. "So much of the feeling of depression," says Moody, "can be traced to the feeling of 'I can't grow' or 'I can't be creative.'"

Psychiatrist Robert N. Butler has discovered that older people begin to undergo a spontaneous resurgence of early memories— something he calls the "life-review process." This review of memories, dismissed for so long as senile flights into the past, is actually "a natural, healthy way of coming to terms with ourselves," Moody explains. "It's a life-affirming process that can integrate one's experience, a process that can be used for learning, for creation."

Marc Kaminsky started the Arts of Elders project for New York City's Teachers and Writers Collaborative in 1979. "The life-review process is the cutting edge where gerontology and the humanities meet," Kaminsky says. Older people's reminiscences can be shaped into journals, poetry, novels and plays.

All this leads to another exercise. Start writing down your experiences, what they have taught you, and how you can apply those experiences to creating a rewarding life. Include interests and talents you might have begun developing as far back as childhood, ambitions you may have abandoned long ago.

It isn't just low self-opinion that stifles many people's creative thinking. Other things thwart our endeavors over the years. The greatest thief of creativity is time—or the lack of it. We're all in danger of being consumed by mindless routine. If you're not working full time, you probably feel compelled to fill up all those "free" hours with household chores, errands, and the like. But what you really need to do is make time to daydream.

Then, you need to foster a truly open mind—that is, a mind free to relax, free of inhibitions. Creative people tend to look at the big picture. They don't allow themselves to be limited by everyday problems; they take care of those efficiently and without procrastination, then move on.

The Proper Mindset

To be all you can be at this stage of life, it is crucial to adopt a new mindset—one that allows fresh ideas to come in, one that filters out negative and stifling restraints on thinking and perspective. Some practical suggestions to help you frame that new mindset:

1. Think positively. Nothing cramps your life more than a negative attitude. ("It's too late," or "life has passed me by.") Think about it: A person in relatively good health at the age of 50 can look forward to at least another 25 years of productive life. That means a full third or more of his/her life is still ahead. A positive person is always looking to the future. He/she imagines, improvises, plans, dreams, and follows through—and is a happier, more capable person because of it.

2. Brainstorm. Take the brakes off your mind. One way to start is to write down one specific thing that would significantly improve each of the following: your life, your family's life, your work environment, your skills, your community. This can be an even more exciting exercise if you get together with several other people whom you respect and with whom you enjoy trading ideas. Have each write down a new thought on a subject of mutual interest. You will be amazed at the number of really good ideas generated from such a session! Remember that Einstein, Fuller, Newton, Monet and the Wright Brothers all used other people's concepts to help them create.

3. Dream. The most effective way to give birth to an idea is to let it come on its own. Some of our most creative moments occur in the middle of the night, so keep a pad on your nightstand to record your thoughts. Take the time to daydream and see how much leaps from your subconscious to your conscious mind.

4. Search. Looking for a better way is part and parcel of progress. Within each individual mind is the mechanism to create ideas, but it takes a little background, a little research. If something interests you, head for the library and read everything you can find on the subject. Ask the experts. If at all possible, go into the field for a first-hand, on-the-spot look.

5. Mingle. Get to know other creative people. They can stimulate you beyond your wildest dreams. Whether you go for a collaboration, a team effort, or just some friendly advice, approach others and exchange ideas.

6. Relax. Don't let yourself be intimidated by all that must go into a new business. Everyone I know who started a successful business was an ordinary person with an idea.

7. Do it. You can have the best ideas in the world, but if you don't do something about them, what good are they? It takes courage and determination to make an idea reality—but you *can* do it!

CHAPTER 5

Prepare for Risk

Perhaps you have always gone out of your way to avoid risk. And when you *were* forced to gamble, you did so with great trepidation. Often someone else (your boss, spouse, a parent, etc.) acted as a buffer between you and that risk. Most people spend the first and second quarters of their lives working for or with others who take the chances. Yet don't we admire and respect those risk-takers, and maybe even dream of being in a position to gamble on our own capabilities?

Risk isn't all that horrible. It requires that you evaluate the situation, recognize and believe in your abilities, then prepare yourself psychologically, emotionally and physically for whatever will happen. A risk-free life can be a prison. People who hang on to dead-end jobs just because they fear starting something new are counterproductive, serving neither themselves nor the people they work for.

In short, don't wait for change to come to you. Make it happen.

There is a fable about a man who avoided risks. At age 15 he fell out of a tree and broke his arm. He never climbed a tree again. At 23 he got food poisoning after a salmon dinner. He never ate seafood again. At 32 the stocks he had purchased five years before ended up worthless. He never invested again. At 42 he was in an automobile accident. He was not injured, but he rarely went out anymore. At 47 his best friend betrayed him in a business deal. He stopped reaching out to people. At 55 he was ready to retire. He made sure there was as little risk in his life as possible. He wouldn't exercise. He watched TV all the time. He was bored. At 60 his health started to deteriorate. He had arteriosclerosis, varicose veins, back problems, indigestion and was 40 pounds overweight. To those around him he was a boring, opinionated, useless human being. Every day he wondered what had happened to his life.

Do you want to be that man?

Get Involved

No matter what your age, you are probably always searching for ways to renew your life, put a new spin on it, make it more interesting. You can find that excitement, that sense of self-fulfillment by starting your own business.

Yes, it involves a big risk. But the risk is a creative and beneficial one. And there are ways to spread it out. Start laying the groundwork for your new business now—before you retire, or while you still have financial backup. Go back to school. Take a few financial courses, learn basic computer operation. Start visiting and researching various types of businesses. Make the time today to plan for your big move into entrepreneurship tomorrow. Take and handle one risk at a time and you will minimize the trauma of going into business cold turkey.

There are many programs that will help you polish your skills so you'll be able to handle all the nuances of your new business with a self-assurance that will surprise you.

Read everything put out by the Small Business Administration and attend its seminars. Check the catalogs of nearby colleges and universities for classes that will help you handle the basics of business (accounting, tax law, marketing, management, etc.). One of the best ways to get in touch with what's happening is to rub elbows with the younger generation.

Colleges and universities aren't the only places to get classes. High school districts all over the country offer adult education

STAY WITH WHAT YOU KNOW.

classes. In rural areas, the local agricultural extension office lists many courses that may be of interest to you. And there are the many institutions that offer specific courses.

Other excellent classes are offered by Elderhostel (80 Boylston, St, Ste 400, Boston, MA 02116). Impressive curricula geared to the older learner take advantage of empty college dormitories and classrooms.

In the unlikely event you can't find a course or class that meets your needs, find other individuals with the same interest and approach your community college officials. Chances are if there are enough prospective students, they will set up a class.

Whatever avenue you choose to begin your risk-taking adventure, remember that the basic mechanism is always the same. A risk is simply taking a chance. It involves leaping from one place, where you are no longer happy, to a new place where you believe things will be better. Also, know that the wisdom of your years will help you know which risks are worthwhile and which are not.

Handling Risk

We all know people who are dissatisfied with their personal lives or careers—or both—yet seem unable to change anything. Either they never learned the art of taking risks, or they have forgotten it. Here are some steps you can take to prepare yourself for taking risk:

1. Cut your losses. Write off what no longer works, get rid of attachments held out of fear. Steep yourself in the positive aspects of your life thus far, reinforcing yourself with instances where you perservered and came out on top. Constantly rid yourself of the baggage that holds negative attitudes, counterproductive thinking and self-defeating notions.

The first step in doing this involves admitting to yourself what is wrong with your worklife. Are you bored with your job? Have you reached a dead end? Have you always disliked your work? Once you truthfully admit the problem to yourself, you will be ready to take the next step. And the risk will be easier to face, because you are taking a chance for a better future.

2. Come to terms with loss. As you've grown older, you've been forced to adapt to inevitable losses: losing a job or promotion to someone else, the death of a loved one or dear friend, selling the family home. Each of these has involved an adjustment period. But it is to be hoped you have learned that for every negative, there is a positive—that you can and must continue to move ahead.

Maybe you are afraid of any type of loss and have hung on to your present job because of its security. You've probably also attached yourself to certain institutions, organizations and people because of their stability. But now that retirement approaches, or is here, you must free yourself so you can move forward. Any farmer or jockey can tell you: If you hold the reins too tightly, the horse won't move at all.

3. Let go. When you jump over a ditch, you first look to be sure your footing on the near side is firm. Then you look for a foothold on the far side. When you are sure of your footholds, you leave one side for the other. A full and active life is filled with similar jumps from one situation to another. With a little planning most of these risks can be carefully calculated so they won't involve any nasty surprises.

Timing is everything. Letting go involves adequate planning for and assessment of how and when risk is to occur. You don't want to risk too early or too late. You don't want to risk too much or too little.

Ellen J. sat down to fill some time while her husband was on a business trip. She made a list of all the things she thought she needed to know so that she could be completely self-sufficient, should the need arise. On her list were such things as knowing what bills were owed and when they were due, learning how to prepare tax returns, having some knowledge of basic car repair, and being able to generate some kind of income.

Then Ellen followed through. Over the next five years she took courses so that she could handle every item on her list. She whizzed through two accounting courses, learned how to complete an income tax return, took a course in basic automobile maintenance, and opened a small clothing shop near her home. Now that her husband has retired he helps her run her three stores and they are both extremely happy with their life. It took a conscious effort for this woman to plan and let go of her complacency. But she wanted to be self-sufficient—and self-sufficient she is.

4. Reach out and find a landing place. As discussed earlier, it's never a good idea to jump a ditch without knowing where you're going to land. It's the same when starting a business. You have to have some qualifications for opening the type of business you choose. You have to be sure that the business you choose is the right one for you.

Landing safely on the other side requires some surveying. Being sure you are going into the right business requires some research and planning. Study the business you want very carefully. Acquire any and all skills you will need to handle the business. You'll find that the fear of starting something new is diminished in direct proportion to how much you know about that something new.

5. Embrace your new environment. Once you've laid your groundwork and made your decision, go with it wholeheartedly. Give 100 percent of yourself to make your venture successful. Don't falter or even let ideas of failure enter your mind. You've made the jump, now make the best of it.

Generally, the risks involved in starting or buying a business are about the same as other risks. However, there are two key differences:

a. Financial. How much can you afford to lose? Don't risk all your money. Risk only what you can afford to lose. If this isn't enough to enter into the business you have chosen, look for partners, additional investors or a business loan. You can't give 100 percent if you're too close to the brink.

b. Personal. Every bit as important as the amount of money you intend to invest in a new business is the amount of time you intend to put into it. Use the same formula. How much time can you really afford to give? Will that be enough to make a go of your new enterprise?

Several years ago, during an appearance on the Phil Donahue show, I was asked by a woman who had just inherited $100,000 how much of it I thought she should risk on a new business. My answer was quick: If you've done all the proper planning and are sure of the direction you're going, risk $10,000 of the money and set aside another $15,000 as an emergency backup. My point was that it's not smart to go for broke; it's far wiser to take a risk from which you can recover should you fail.

Where the Mistakes Are

My years of working as a business consultant put me in close touch with many types of businesses that were on the verge of going under. From my vantage point I could see where mistakes were made. My findings:

1. **Investing money unwisely.** This usually involved paying too high a price for goodwill and investing too much up front in inventory.

2. **Taking on partners with no experience.** The only thing a partner with no experience contributes is his/her money and friendship. (Incidentally, if you lose the money, you usually lose the friendship, too.)

3. **Selecting the wrong location.** If you don't have the proper traffic and visibility, you're doomed before you even open.

4. **Paying too much for rent.** Why work for the landlord?

5. Investing too much initially in furniture and fixtures. This is an ego thing and one of the easiest traps to fall into. Start with the minimum; add new things as the business grows and prospers.

6. Failing to have a proper business plan. From the start you should have a detailed plan of where you intend to go.

7. Underfinancing. Underestimating the costs of starting a business is one of the biggest mistakes you can make. Many failed businesses would have succeeded had their owners been able to hold on for another six months.

8. Neglecting initial research. You have to know who and where your competition is and will be.

9. Settling for a high interest rate on borrowed capital. This mistake can eat your business alive.

10. Being unable to control operating costs. You have to know where every penny is going at all times. If you haven't planned for every contingency, you could be wiped out.

11. Underpricing. Don't be afraid to charge what your product or service is worth. Know the going rate for what you provide, and put your charge in that ballpark.

12. Ignoring the need for good customer relations. Word of mouth is the quickest, least expensive—and best—advertising.

13. Neglecting to promote your business or maintain a good public image. "Early to bed, early to rise, work like hell and advertise!"

14. Hesitating to make decisions and act on them. All the plans in the world are for naught if they aren't acted upon.

15. Failing to know every job in your organization. Never be dependent on anyone to carry out a job. If you are, one sick employee or one who quits can send you into bankruptcy.

16. Thinking you can do it all. Retain the services of professional accountants, lawyers, etc. Trying to cut corners by not paying for professional support is a good way to cut your own throat.

17. Failing to allow for taxes. This will eat up your capital and profits.

18. Underinsuring your company. All it will take is one accident, fire or other problem to send you into bankruptcy.

19. Inadequately training your personnel. This is one of the quickest ways to assure poor sales and low volume.

20. Underestimating your competition. Knowing who they are isn't enough. You have to offer more than they do.

21. Getting too complacent. Never sit back and take your success for granted. There's always someone out there just waiting for the opportunity to go a little further and take away your business.

22. Failing to recognize new market trends. Stay on top of the market. Know what's coming down the pike. If you don't, the industry will pass you by.

23. Maintaining insufficient working capital. This saps your business' strength until there's nothing left.

24. Budgeting badly. Red ink will flow.

25. Issuing too much credit. Unless your new business is banking, leave that to someone else.

26. Having insufficient financial data. If you can't keep track of every penny, you're taking unnecessary risks.

27. Lacking proper collection procedures. If a customer owes you money, go after him/her. If you don't have the time, hire a collection agency and an attorney.

28. Borrowing too much capital. This can put an additional burden on your business you don't need.

29. Losing control of accounts receivable. Bill on time and send second notices on time. Accounts receivable are the life blood of your company.

30. Failing to control accounts payable. Take advantage of every cash discount and primary line you can. Keep detailed records—and pay your bills on time.

WHAT KIND OF BUSINESS DO YOU WANT?

Business Facts Almanac

"If you have a lemon, make lemonade."
—Howard Gossard

"In the long run, men hit only what they aim at."
—Henry David Thoreau

Now that you've taken a thorough inventory of your talents and skills, it's time to match them with a business. The chapters in this section are designed to help you with this task. But before we match you to a business, take a look at the worksheets in this section. They will prove an invaluable aid in helping you set your goals and define your purpose.

Personal Evaluation

Step 1: Identify your strengths and weaknesses.

Owning and running a successful business is a challenge in itself, as we have cautioned. A great many technical, management and personal skills must come into play. With this in mind, fill out the following questionnaire as a way to help identify your strengths and weaknesses.

a. What are your strengths in terms of your technical skills? (Examples: Can you type, use a computer, deal with buying guides, understand a profit/loss statement, operate a cash register?)

_____

_____

_____

b. What are your weaknesses in terms of technical skills?

_____

_____

c. What are your management strengths?

_____

_____

d. What are your management weaknesses?

_____

_____

e. What are your strong personal characteristics?

_____

_____

_____

f. What are your weak personal characteristics?

_____

_____

g. How will you compensate for identified weaknesses?

technical: _____

management: _____

personal: _____

Step 2: Should I own my own business?

	Yes	No
Do you have good health?	_____	_____
Do you plan ahead?	_____	_____
Are you prepared to lose the money you invest in the business?	_____	_____
Are you a leader?	_____	_____

Can you make decisions?   _____   _____

Do you have any business training?   _____   _____

Are you competitive?   _____   _____

Do you get things done on time?   _____   _____

Are you a self-starter?   _____   _____

Are you a good organizer?   _____   _____

Can you live without taking money from
the business for the first year?   _____   _____

Do you adapt well to change?   _____   _____

Are you confident?   _____   _____

Are you aware that many business
owners work 68–80 hours a week?   _____   _____

Do you stick with a project until it is
completed?   _____   _____

Do you have work experience in the
type of business you are considering?   _____   _____

Scoring the above test cannot tell you whether or not you should be in business, but it should give you some areas to consider. A "yes" answer to any question should be considered a good indication and a "no" answer indicates a potential problem area. Think carefully about any "no" answers, and determine how you will deal with problems that may arise. After reviewing the results of this exercise ask yourself one final question: Would you be better off working for someone else? Do not be discouraged by the "no" answers; use them as a guideline to the areas you must put the most work into, or to areas of your business that you may want to turn over to other, more experienced, people.

Goal Setting

Determining your goals is a difficult and often frustrating process. It is, however, a very important step in planning your business. The following exercise is intended to help you clarify your goals, both business and personal. Establishing goals gives you a yardstick to measure your performance as you progress through life. Goals are very personal—there are no right or wrong answers. Only you can determine what goals are appropriate.

Step 1: Define long-term goals.

a. What are your lifetime goals?

_____

_____

_____

b. What are your goals for the next 25 years?

_____

_____

_____

Step 2: Define intermediate-term goals.

a. What are your goals for the next seven years?

_____

_____

_____

b. What are your goals for the next three years?

_____

_____

_____

Step 3: Define short-term goals.

a. What are your goals for the next year?

_____

_____

_____

b. What would be your goals if you had one year left to live?

_____

_____

_____

Step 4: Define your business goals.

Review the business and personal goals listed in the first three steps and select business goals that are compatible with your personal goals.

a. What are your long-term goals for this business?

_____

_____

_____

b. What are your five-year goals for this business?

_____

_____

_____

c. What are your one-year goals for this business?

_____

_____

_____

Purpose of the Business

Step 1: Identify purposes of your business plan.

Your first important decision is to clearly define the purposes of writing this business plan. It may be to obtain financing, to serve as a guide for managing your business, to help you clarify all aspects of your business, or even to help you make a final decision about starting your own business at all.

a. Who will use your business plan?
b. What do you hope to accomplish with this written plan?

Purpose of business plan:

_____

_____

_____

_____

_____

Step 2: Define the overall purposes of your business.

The section on goals has helped prepare you for these steps. In this step you need to identify business and personal reasons for your business endeavor. The overall purpose should be long-term and general in nature.

a. What are the main personal purposes for this business?
b. What are the main business purposes for this business?
c. Are the combined personal and business purposes compatible?

Overall purpose of business:

_____

_____

_____

_____

_____

_____

_____

_____

Step 3: Identify specific goals aimed at overall purposes.

Now you have identified both the personal and business purposes for your business. You must also identify specific goals that will be steps toward accomplishing your overall objectives. Goals are definitive statements of what you want to happen. Each should include when you will reach the goal and a way to measure it. Some of the major goals, both personal and business, are addressed in this exercise. Avoid conflicts among various goals. All should point toward the accomplishment of your overall objectives.

a. What are your goals for the growth of sales volume?
b. What are your goals for profit before taxes?
c. What are your goals for compensations for effort?

d. What are your goals for time you will commit?

e. What are your goals for personal growth and education?

f. What are your other goals?

Specific goals of the business:

_____

_____

_____

_____

_____

_____

_____

_____

_____

_____

_____

_____

_____

_____

CHAPTER 6

Shopping for a Business

Now that you've assessed your personal, professional and potential professional assets, let's explore the various types of businesses there are and determine how to find the one that's right for you.

When choosing a business, there are myriad factors to consider: your skills, talents, experiences and interests as well as your health and family commitments. If you weigh all of them carefully, you can pick the business that best meshes with your unique personal profile.

What follows is a rundown of the most profitable businesses, courtesy of the American Entrepreneur Association.

Animal-oriented business: Pet supplies, pet hotel and grooming, pet cemetery, aquarium fish and supplies.

Apparel businesses: Costume jewelry, women's apparel, intimate apparel, children's clothing, men's apparel, Western wear, consignment/used clothing.

Automotive businesses: 30-minute tune-ups, consignment car sales, do-it-yourself auto repairs, mufflers, auto-parking service, auto painting, 10-minute oil changes, self-service gas station, car wash, vinyl-repair service, rent-a-used-car agency, automobile detailing, propane-conversion center, auto parts, sheepskin seat-covers, used battery reclaiming, car stereo installation.

Craft businesses: Art show promotion, custom rugmaking, hot tub manufacturing and sales, bonsai supplies, stained-glass window manufacturing, burlwood table manufacturing and sales,

"I'VE BEEN MEANING TO ASK, ARE WE GETTING BORED WITH THIS GAME?"

handcrafts co-op gallery, sculptured candlemaking, do-it-yourself framing, handcraft manufacturing, craft success manual, balloon bouquet service.

Education-oriented businesses: Bartender/waitress school, teacher's agency, used books, home tutoring.

Services to the home: Window-washing service, tool and equipment rental, furniture stripping/refinishing, carpet-cleaning service, kitchen cabinet facelifting, chimney-sweep service, maid service, lawn care/gardening, firewood sales, catering, wallpapering, porcelain refinishing.

Fast-food business: Pizzeria, fried chicken takeout restaurant, mobile restaurant/sandwich truck, hot dog/hamburger stand, frozen yogurt, chocolate-chip cookies, doughnuts, frystick snacks, pasta.

Home-based businesses: Mail-order sales, flea market and swap meet promotion, worm farming, importing and exporting.

Home furnishings: Furniture, mattresses, paint and wall-coverings, furniture rental, oriental rugs and auction, waterbeds, used carpeting, consignment used furniture, antique ceiling fans.

Improving your business ability: SBA financing—new businesses, SBA financing—existing businesses, promotional gimmicks, how to develop multilevel marketing and sales, how to obtain government contracts, entrepreneurs institute (correspondence course), complete library of all manuals, how to raise the money you need, how to intelligently buy a business, how to develop a business plan to ensure success, analysis and rating of all franchises, incorporation kits for any state.

Energy-related businesses: Energy-loss-prevention consultancy and sales, plastics-recycling center, insulation contracting, used paper collecting and recycling, one-stop energy sales, solar sales and installation, oil well development.

Tourist businesses: Dive-for-a-pearl shop, computer handwriting analysis, T-shirts, shells, license-plate-frame engraving.

Miscellaneous retail businesses: Plants/flowers, adult book-store, antiques, sunglasses, computers, gift shop/boutique, pipes, discount fabrics, gourmet cookware, telephones, wedding shop, survival store, optical products, religious gifts, heart specialty store.

Employment services: Employment agency, temporary-help service, computer consulting and temporary help service, executive recruiting service.

Miscellaneous service businesses: Dry-cleaning, mini warehouse, day-care center, digital watch repair service, private mailbox service, security patrol service, coin laundry, mobile locksmithing, gift-wrapping and mailing service.

Personal services: Roommate-finding service; do-it-yourself cosmetic shop, family hair salon, tanning center, dating service.

Photography-oriented businesses: Antique photo shop, photocopying service, keychain photos, videotaping service, one-hour photo processing lab.

Publishing businesses: Rental information publishing, "Who's Who" directory publishing, newsletter publishing, free classified-ads newspaper.

Recreation and entertainment businesses: Adults-only motel, pinball and video game arcade, no-alcohol bar, hobby shop, travel agency, video store, hot-tub rental, bar/disco/tavern/nightclub, videocassette rental.

Retail food and spirits: Cheese, wine and gourmet food shop, liquor store, lo-cal baked-goods, homemade cakes, health foods, specialty breads, vitamin-nutrition store, convenience foods, candy and chocolate shop, coffees and teas.

Self-improvement businesses: No-smoking clinic, psychic-training seminars, weight-control clinic, physical-fitness center, aerobic dance studio.

Services to businesses: Instant print shop, parking lot striping and maintenance service, rent-a-plant service, voice-stress/lie-detector service, liquidator selling distressed merchandise, coin-op

TVs, secretarial service, telephone-answering service, mobile surface cleaning, consulting business, cross-country trucking, bartering club, collection agency, advertising, limousine service, used restaurant-grease collection service, coupon mailer service, apartment preparation service, typesetting service, financial broker.

Restaurants: Coffee shop, salads only, soups only, sandwich shop, stuffed-potatoes, old-fashioned ice cream parlor, omelette shop, Mexican (or other foreign cuisine) restaurant.

Street-vending businesses: Balloons, flowers, popcorn, handmade ice cream bars.

Sports businesses: Tennis and racquetball club, athletic shoe store, bicycle shop, roller-skate rental, roller-skating rink and skateboard park, windsurfing sales and school, backpacking shop, sailboard time-share leasing, mo-ped shop, sports forecasting service, sunken golf ball recovery.

Unusual businesses: Contest promoting, seminar promoting, burglar-alarm sales, Christmas tree lot and ornament shop, flat-fee real estate company, jojoba plantation, gold prospecting, safe-deposit-box rental center.

If you haven't decided what business you are suited for, check this list especially developed for entrepreneurs over 50.

Small Business Shopping List

Accounting & tax service	Auto supply store
Address & mailing house	Automobile rentals
Advertising service	Babysitting service
Alterations	Beauty salon
Answering service	Bookkeeping service
Antique store	Bookstore
Art gallery	Business consultancy
Art supplies	Cake baking
Arts & crafts gallery	Candy store

Carpentry repair	House painting
Carpet cleaning	Ice cream parlor
Carwash	Laundry & dry cleaner
Catering service	Limousine service
Computer service	Machine repairs
Convenience food store	Mail-order sales
Credit & collection service	Men's or women's specialty store
Day-care center	Messenger service
Diet center	Miniature golf course
Door-to-door sales	Modeling
Dry cleaning	Motel
Employment agency	Party planning
Engraving	Pet store
Equipment leasing	Picture framing
Fire & theft alarm systems	Printing service
Furniture repair	Publishing (newsletters, etc.)
Gardening service	Quilting & needlework business
Gift shop	Secretarial & typing service
Golf driving range	Shopping service
Gourmet food store	Sports store
Hair service	Stained-glass manufacturer
Hardware (self-service)	Taxi service
Health club	Teaching (music, art, sewing,
Health-food store	writing, crafts, etc.)
Health transportation service	Temporary help agency
Hobby shop	Tutoring
Home maid service	Upholstery
Home nursing	Vinyl repair
Home product sales	Word processing

CHAPTER 7

The Franchise Option

Franchise is one of America's most popular entrepreneurial activities. It is estimated by the United States Department of Commerce that there are almost 500,000 franchise outlets. John Naisbitt, author of *MegaTrends*, says that by the year 2000 at least half of all retail sales outlets will be franchises.

The popularity of franchises revolves around the fact that they come with a proven business plan. In addition, there is some follow-up supervision provided after the business is started.

Even though there are hundreds, if not thousands, of legitimate franchise companies across the country, the word is still "buyer beware." This because many unscrupulous companies have bilked millions of dollars from would-be franchisees by selling illegal or nonexistent franchises.

One example: A company offered franchises for a senior newspaper. Everything looked perfect and professional. Prospective franchisees thought this was an excellent opportunity to tap into a specialized market for a minimal amount of money. But those who put their money down ended up with only a book on how to start a newspaper.

Sometimes when individuals buy a franchise they end up with little more than a name. Remember, as a franchisee you have a right to expect a continuing relationship in which the franchiser provides a licensed privilege to do business, plus assistance in organizing, training, merchandising and managing the establishment.

A FRANCHISE IS A BUSINESS ALREADY PACKAGED TO GO.

Buying a franchise doesn't mean you can operate without any business experience, however. A franchise requires just as much know-how as any other kind of business. What it does offer is a little more structure and, usually, an already accepted product or service.

More advantages of franchising:

- The name is already established.
- The company has identification in your market.
- Through the franchiser you establish immediate credit.
- Your lease, insurance, training, merchandise, purchasing and profit-and-loss statements are taken care of by the franchiser.
- The business research has been done.

However, there are also concerns you should address:

- Thoroughly check the reputation and financial standing of the franchiser.
- Make sure your market area can support the franchise you are interested in.
- Consult an attorney before signing any agreement.
- Make a careful assessment of both growth and obsolescence factors of the product or service.
- Have your own accountant review all statements and other paperwork that comes from the franchiser.

Doing Your Franchise Homework

With some idea of the strengths and weaknesses of franchises, you can start your search for one that would work best for you. The following guidelines, developed by the Council of Better Business Bureaus, will help you make a prudent choice. Follow each step carefully before buying into a franchise.

Generalities

- Collect general information on both the franchise and the product or service it offers. Extend your search over several months, using as many independent sources as you can.
- Double- and triple-check everything the company tells you with an unbiased independent source.
- Keep a written record of all your conversations, meetings and transactions with the franchiser.

Company Background

- Check out the corporate name. Are you paying your franchise fee to a separate corporation set up specifically to sell franchises or to the founding company? Beware of professional franchise salesmen brought in only to sell as many franchises as possible in the shortest time. There may be no continuing relationship—yet that is essential to a successful franchise.
- Research how long the franchiser has been in business. How long selling franchises? How many franchises sold in each of the last five years? Of these, how many are still operated by their original purchasers?
- Find out who the firm's principals are and what businesses they were associated with in each of the last ten years. Get company names, addresses and check them out. Are the principals experienced in this type of business or are they only specialists in franchise sales?
- Know the franchiser's financial situation. Get a copy of the annual report and certified financial statements. Check banking references, trade creditor references and the franchiser's line of credit with financial institutions. How long have these financial arrangements been in existence? Longevity is very important. (If you don't understand the language of finance, consult a professional. For instance, would you understand what it meant if the bank told you

a firm had a "medium four-figure balance, non-borrowing account?" It sounds good, but what it means is that the firm has between $3,000 and $7,000 in its account and the bank does not extend credit to it.

    • Know what the franchiser's plans for future development are. Are those plans in writing? Do they appear reasonable in light of recent expansion and existing management and financial resources?

    • Check with the Better Business Bureau. However, don't be lulled by the fact that the company has no complaints filed against it. That is only relevant if the company has been in business in the local area for several years. Most franchise complaints never surface, and if they do it is often two years or more after the original cash outlay.

    • Check the franchiser's state license. See if your state laws require a franchiser to register and provide a disclosure statement to potential franchisees. If your state does not require licensing, check out the franchiser's status in a nearby state that does. But don't drop your guard just because the franchiser is licensed.

    • Find out what requirements the franchiser set up for prospective franchisees. Ask for the names and addresses of existing franchisees. Talk to them.

Questions to Ask—and Answer

About the Product or Service:
    • Is the quality good? Excellent? How does the franchiser's product or service compare with others of the same type?

    • Is the product or service a staple? A fad? A luxury? If it's a fad, will it be a bestseller long enough for you to get your money *and* a profit out of it? If it's a staple, is there enough demand to sustain it? If it's seasonal, will you be ready to tap the first major selling season shortly after you open?

- How well is the product or service selling now? How did it sell in the recent past? Over the past few years? How long has it been on the market in your area? In other areas?
    - Is it priced competitively and packaged attractively?
    - Where and how great is the competition? (Mark an area map with the location of all your competitors.)
    - What is the product's or service's reputation? (Ask friends, family and associates what they think of it.)

About the Territory:
- Is the franchise territory well defined?
- What are the provisions for territorial protection?
- Is the territory large enough to generate continued sales?

About the Future:
- Is there potential for growth?
- What is the maximum projected annual income?
- Are there seasonal income fluctuations?
- How are similar nearby franchises doing?

About the Contract:
- Does the contract cover all claims, written and oral, from both parties?
    - Are the benefits to and obligations of both parties balanced?
    - Can the contract be renewed, terminated or transferred? Under what circumstances?
    - Under what conditions can the franchise be lost?
    - What size and type of operation is specified?
    - Is there an additional fixed payment each year?
    - Is there a percent-of-gross-sales payment?
    - Must a certain amount of the merchandise be purchased? From whom?
    - Is there an annual sales quota?
    - Can the franchisee return merchandise for credit?

- Can the franchisee engage in other business activities?
- Is there a franchise fee? Is it equitable?
- Have you had a lawyer experienced with franchises examine the contract? An accountant?

About Franchiser Support:
- Does the franchiser provide continuing assistance?
- Is training available for franchisees and key employees?
- Are a manual, sales kit, and accounting system provided?
- Does the franchiser select store location? Is there a fee?
- Does the franchiser handle lease arrangements?
- Does the franchiser design store layout and displays?
- Does the franchiser select opening inventory?
- Does the franchiser provide inventory-control methods?
- Does the franchiser provide market surveys?
- Does the franchiser help analyze financial statements?
- Does the franchiser provide purchasing guides?

If you take all of the preceding steps and get answers to all of the questions, you will not only have an excellent idea of what type of business you are undertaking, you also will be better prepared should something go wrong.

Jim and Olga Peterson were extremely careful when they purchased their franchise. They did all their homework, including contacting other franchisees in the area. They located their business in a mall and operated it very successfully for more than a year. Then their national franchiser went bankrupt. Because the mall would not allow any business that was not connected with a nationally recognized concern to operate, they were asked to move out. However, because the Petersons had established a working relationship with fellow franchisees under the bankrupt franchiser they were able to get together and work out a loose business association—which allowed all of them to remain in their chosen locations.

Finding Your Franchise

There are a multitude of ways to start shopping for your franchise. Franchise expositions and fairs are held regularly all over the country. There are also a host of consumer and referral groups, and several annuals and franchise directories are published. In short, shopping for a franchise is almost as easy as shopping for a new car.

Various financial publications have regular sections that rate and provide updates on franchise companies. A good place to start is your local library.

For detailed information on many franchise companies contact the International Franchise Association, 1350 New York Ave NW, Ste 900, Washington, DC 20005. Call (202) 628–8000.

Two other sources are *The Franchise Annual*, Info Press Inc., 728 Center St, Box 550, Lewiston, NY 14092-0580 and the *Directory of Franchising Organizations*, Pilot Industries, Inc., 103 Cooper St, New York, NY 11702.

Where to Start

The following list is not an endorsement. It is presented strictly as a starting point for your exploration of the vast range of products and services available through franchises at comparatively low starting costs (under $50,000).

But once again: Should you seriously consider purchasing any of the franchises on this list, be sure to follow all the investigative steps we have previously outlined.

OWNING A FRANCHISE IS LIKE SOMEONE
STANDING BEHIND YOU IN BUSINESS.

Accounting and Tax Services

H & R Block Inc.: 4410 Main St., Kansas City, MO 64111.

Jackson Hewit Tax Service: 6513 College Park Square, Virginia Beach, VA 23464. Contact: Carolyn Buzek.

Tax Man Inc: 674 Massachusetts Ave, Cambridge, MA 02139.

Advertising Services

American Advertising Distributors: 234 S Extension, Mesa, AZ 85201.

ESP Co-Op: 195 Cortlandt St, Belleville, NJ 07109.

Headlines USA: 2401 Fountainview, Houston, TX 77057.

Homes & Land Magazine: 2365 Centerville Rd, Tallahassee, FL 32308.

K & O Publishing, Inc: 7522-20th NE, Seattle, WA 98115.

Mr. Sign: 159 Keyland Ct, Bohemia, NY 11716.

Money Stretchers: 6799 Parma Park, Cleveland, OH 44130.

Pennysaver: 80 Eighth Ave, New York, NY 10011.

Rooftop Balloons: 10770 Rockville, Ste B, Santee, CA 92071.

Signs Now: 660 Azalea, Mobile, AL 36609.

Stuffit Direct Mktg: 12450 Automobile Blvd, Clearwater, FL 34622.

Super Coups: 11 Tosca Dr, Stoughton, MA 02072.

TBS Advertising Centers: Drawer D, Beach Lake, PA 18405.

TV Facts: 1638 New Highway, Farmingdale, NY 11735.

TV Scene: 11641 Marshwood Ln SW, Fort Myers, FL 33908.

Automobile Rental & Leasing

Affordable Used Car Rental System, Inc.: 88A West Front St, Keyport, NJ 07735.

All Star Rent-a-Car: Box 69027, Seattle, WA 98168.

American Safari National RV Rental System: 420 Lincoln Rd, Ste 316, Miami Beach, FL 33139.

Rent-a-Wreck: 1100 Glendon Ave, Ste 1250, Los Angeles, CA 90024.

Ugly Duckling Rent-a-Car System, Inc.: 7750 Broadway, Ste 100, Tucson, AZ 85710.

Automotive Lubrication & Tune Up

5-Minute Oil Change, Inc.: 366 Columbia St, Utica, NY 13502.

Jiffy Lube International, Inc.: 6000 Metro Dr., Baltimore, MD 21215.

The Lube Wagon: 9430 Mission Blvd, Riverside, CA 92509.

U.S.A. Fastlube Systems, Inc.: 274 Union, Lakewood, CO 80228.

Automotive Muffler Shops

Quick-O Muffler Centers: 1490 Interstate Dr, Cookeville, TN 38501.

Scotti Muffler Centers: 5959 E Rosedale, Fort Worth, TX 76112.

Automotive Products & Services

AAMCO Transmissions, Inc.: 1 Presidential Blvd., Bala Cynw Yd, PA 19004.

ABC Mobile Brake Services: 18 Crawford St, Needham Heights, MA 02194.

American Mobile Wash: 4141 Sayles Blvd, Abilene, TX 79602.

Chem-Glass Windshield Repair: 7111 Ohms Lane, Minneapolis, MN 55435.

CleanCo, Inc.: 8018 Sunnyside Rd, Minneapolis, MN 55432.

Dr. Vinyl & Associates: 3001 Cherry St, Kansas City, MO 64108.

Jiffiwash, Inc.: 1177 California St, Ste 308, San Francisco, CA 94108.

Property Damage Appraisers: 6100 Western Pl, Ste 900, PO Box 9230, Fort Worth, TX 76107.

Sparkle Wash, Inc.: 26851 Richmond Rd, Cleveland, OH 44146.

Tidy Car, Inc.: 1515 N Federal Hwy, PO Box 1589, Boca Raton, FL 33429.

Triex: 125 Parkway, Ste 10, Bronkville, NY 10708.

Automotive Transmission Repair

Cottman Transmission Center: 240 New York Dr, Fort Washington, PA 19034.

Beverages

Mountain Valley Spring Co.: PO Box 1610, Hot Springs, AR 71902.

Building Products & Homeowner Services

Armstrong World Industries: PO Box 3001, Lancaster, PA 17604.

Bathcrest, Inc.: 2425 S Progress Dr, Salt Lake City, UT 84119.

CAHS, Inc.: 550 S Columbus Ave, Mount Vernon, NY 10550.

Caribbean Clear, Inc.: Rt 3 Box 147, Brodie Rd, Leesville, SC 29070.

Consumer Energy Savers: 1040 Kings Hwy N, Ste 600, Cherry Hill, NJ 08034.

Curbmate Corp.: 5505 S 900 E, Ste 200, Salt Lake City, UT 84117.

Decowall: 5413 Rhea Ave, Tarzana, CA 91356.

Dial One International, Inc.: 4100 Long Beach Blvd, Long Beach, CA 90807.

Dictograph Security Systems: 26 Columbia Turnpike, Florham Park, NJ 07932.

Eureka Log Homes, Inc.: Box 426, Berryville, AR 72616.

Fire Defense Centers: 3919 Morton St, Jacksonville, FL 32217.

Fire Protection USA, Inc.: 1787 E Fort Union Blvd, Ste 201, Salt Lake City, UT 84121.

Porcelain Patch & Glaze Co.: 140 Watertown St, Watertown, MA 02172.

Roto-Rooter Corp.: 300 Ashworth Rd, West Des Moines, IA 50265.

The Security Alliance Corp.: 1865 Miner St, Des Plaines, IL 60016.

Yellowstone Log Homes: 280 N Yellowstone, Rigby, ID 83442.

Business Products & Homeowner Services

Actionfax: 6390 LBJ Fwy, Dallas, TX 75240.

American Lenders Service: PO Box 4855, Odessa, TX 79760.

Associated Air Freight, Inc.: 3333 New Hyde Park Rd, New Hyde Park, NY 11042.

Baby-tenda Corp.: 123 S Belmont, Kansas City, MO 64123.

Barter Exchange, Inc.: 1106 Clayton Lane, Ste 480 W, Austin, TX 78723.

BX International: 5015 Eagle Rock Blvd, Ste 100, PO Box 41912, Los Angeles, CA 90041.

Binex Business Services: 1787 Tribute Rd, Ste M, Sacramento, CA 95815.

Business Data Services, Inc.: 5225 Katy Fwy, Ste 100, Houston, TX 77007.

Business Group of America: 3514 Westford Dr, Tallahassee, FL 32303.

Cashland Corporation: 451 2nd St, Solvang, CA 93111.

Chem-dry Carpet & Upholstery Cleaning (Harris Research Inc.): 3330 Cameron Park, CA 95682.

Communications World International: 14828 W 6th Ave, Unit 13B, Golden, CO 80401–5045.

Copymat: 2000 Powell, Emeryville, CA 94608.

Create-A Book: 6380 Euclid Rd, Cincinnati, OH 45236.

Duraclean International, Inc.: 2151 Waukegan Rd, Deerfield, IL 60015.

Edwin K. Williams & Co. (EKW Systems): 5324 Ekwill St, Santa Barbara, CA 93111.

General Business Services, Inc.: 20271 Goldenrod Lane, Germantown, MD 20874.

Guarantee Carpet Cleaning & Dyeing Company: 2953 Powers Ave, Jacksonville, FL 32207.

Handle With Care Packaging Store: 8480 E Orchard Rd, Ste 4900, Englewood, CO 80111.

Homer's Club (Development Services, Inc.): 2 S Carroll St, Madison, WI 53708.

ISU International: PO Box 2822, San Francisco, CA 94126.

Mail Boxes Etc., USA: 556 Oberlin Dr, Ste 100, San Diego, CA 92121.

Marcoin Business Services: 1924 Cliff Valley Way NE, Atlanta, GA 30329.

Mind Games for Thinking Kids (Leisure Learning Products, Inc.): 16 Division St W, PO Box 4869, Greenwich, CT 06830.

Package Shippers, Inc.: PO Box 82184, Tampa, FL 33682.

Packy The Shipper (Pack 'N Ship, PNS, Inc.): 409 Maine St, Racine, WI 53403.

Priority Management Systems: 2401 Gateway Dr, Ste 115, Irving, TX 75063.

Rainbow International Carpet Dyeing & Cleaning: 1010 N University Parks Dr, Waco, TX 76707.

Stanley Steemer Carpet Cleaner: 5500 Stanley Steemer Parkway, Dublin, OH 43017.

Telecheck Services, Inc.: 7510 W Mississippi Ave, Ste 100, PO Box 26140, Lakewood, CO 80226.

Video Data Services: 24 Grove St, Pittsford, NY 14534.

Wee Win Toys & Accessories, Inc.: 15340 Vantage Parkway, E Ste 250, Houston, TX 77032.

Candy Shops

Calico Cottage Candies, Inc.: 393 Sagemore Ave, Mineola, NY 11501.

Frontier Fruit & Nut: 3823 Wadsworth Rd, Norton, OH 44203.

Cleaning Services

Classy Maids USA, Inc.: Ste 202, Acewood Blvd, Madison, WI 53714.

Dial-A-Maid (D. M. Coughlin, Inc.): 753 Harry L. Dr, Johnson City, NY 13790.

Domesticade: 6400 W 100th, Ste 205, Overland Park, KS 66211.

Jani-King: 4950 Keller Springs, Ste 190, Dallas, TX 75248.

Maid Brigade Services: PO Box 1901, Lilburn, GA 30226.

Merry Maids, Inc.: 11117 Mill Valley Rd, Omaha, NE 68154.

Mini Maid Services International: 1855 Piedmont Rd, Ste 100, Marietta, GA 30066.

Molly Maid: 707 Wolverine Tower, 3001 S State St, Ann Arbor, MI 48104.

Servopro Industries, Inc.: 575 Airport Blvd, Gallatin, TN 37066.

Stanley Steemer International: 5500 Stanley Steemer Parkway, Dublin, OH 43017.

Distributors

A.S.P. International, Inc.: (American Safety Products Div.), PO Box 4200, Cleveland, TN 37311.

International Entertainment Systems: (United Ventures, Inc.), PO Box 180, Richmond, IL 60071.

International Home Shopper (American Security Financial): 42 Worthington Access Dr, St Louis, MO 63043.

International Photo Products: 42 Worthington Access Dr, St Louis, MO 63043.

Mechanical Servants, Inc.: 4615 N Clifton Ave, Chicago, IL 60640.

Niagara Cyclo Massage: (Niagra Therapy Manufacturing Corp.), PO Box 1100, Stanley, NC 28164.

Olympic Gold Sporting Products: 421 Franklin St, Schenectady, NY 12305.

Westrock Ice Cream: 1565-D Fifth Industrial Court, Bayshore, NY 11706.

Employment and Personnel

AAA Employment Franchise, Inc.: 410 Creekside Dr, Clearwater, FL 34620.

Best Resume Service: Best Executive Marketing, Ste 1870, 3 Gateway Centre, Pittsburgh, PA 15222.

Compusearch: (Management Recruiters International, Inc.), 1127 Euclid Ave, Ste 1400, Cleveland, OH 44115.

Homewatch Corporation: 2865 S Colorado Blvd, Denver, CO 80222.

Manpower Temporary Services: 5301 N Ironwood Rd, Milwaukee, WI 53201.

Remedy Temp: 32122 Camino Capistrano, San Juan Capistrano, CA 92675.

Sara Care Services: 1200 Golden Key Cir, Ste 368, El Paso, TX 79925.

Sitters Unlimited: 23015 Del Lago, D2–118, Laguna Hills, CA 92653.

Snelling and Snelling: 4000 S Tamiami Trail, Sarasota, FL 33581.

Western Temporary Services, Inc.: 301 Lennon Lane, Walnut Creek, CA 94598.

Entertainment

Complete Music: 8317 Cass St, Omaha, NE 68114.

Gus The Party Bus: (Gus Enterprises), 4 South Ave, Edmond, OK 73103.

Party Time: 395-94th Ave NW, Coon Rapids, MN 55433.

Food: Convenience Stores, Specialty Shops & Supermarkets

A&W Restaurants, Inc.: 17197 N Laurel Dr, Livonia, MI 48152.

Big Orange Franchise, Inc.: PO Box 2620, Fort Walton Beach, FL 32549.

Breaktime, Inc.: 11616 Kaw Dr, Kansas City, KS 66111.

Canteen Corp.: 222 N LaSalle St, Chicago, IL 60610.

Carter's Nuts, Inc.: 215 W 34th St, New York, NY 10001.

Chez Chocolate (Specialty Retail Concepts): PO Box 11025, Winston-Salem, NC 27116.

Convenient Food Marts (Convenient Industries of America, Inc.): 9701 W Higgins Rd, Rosemont, IL 60018.

Dairy Mart Convenience Stores: 240 South Rd, Enfield, CT 06082.

Li'l Peach Convenience Food Stores: 101 Billerica Office Park N, Billerica, MA 01862.

Food: Donut, Bakery & Cookie Shops

Cinnabon: 936 N 34th, Seattle, WA 98103.

Chicago Cinnamon Co.: 10 S Wabash, Chicago, IL 60603.

The Donut Man (American Food Lines, Inc.): 9851 13th Ave N, Minneapolis, MN 55441.

Grandma Love's Cookies and Company: 3600 Atlanta Hwy, Athens, GA 30610.

Paradise Donut Shops: 211 Thompson Blvd, Sedalia, MO 65301.

Food: Ice Cream & Yogurt

Hawaiian Freeze: 222 E Hutchinson, Ste L, San Marcos, TX 78666.

Mister Softee, Inc.: PO Box 313, Runnemede, NJ 08078.

Sno Shack: PO Box 7944, Salt Lake City, UT 84107.

2001 Flavours Ice Cream, Yogurt & Smoothies (Multi-Flavor Ice Cream Machine Co., Inc.): 9555 Owensmouth, Chatsworth, CA 91311.

Food: Restaurants & Quick Service

Boz Hot Dogs: 770 E 142nd St, Dolton, IL 60419.

Brown Bag Deli: 701 Smithfield St, Ste 400, Pittsburgh, PA 15222.

Dairy Sweet Corp.: PO Box 2592, Des Moines, IA 50315.

Dog Days of America: 5571 Peachtree Rd, Chamblee, GA 30341.

Fox's Pizza Den: 122 Carrie Ann Dr, New Kensington, PA 15068.

Golden Chicken Franchises: 3810 W National Ave, Milwaukee, WI 53215.

Ken's Pizza Parlours: 4441 SE 72nd, Tulsa, OK 74145.

Mobile Chef: 1900 W Country Rd C, St. Paul, MN 55113.

Pizza Inn: 2930 Stemmon Fwy, Dallas, TX 75247.

Pizza To Go: 1831 E Mission, Spokane, WA 99202.

Real Pit Bar-B-Q, Inc.: 1680 Dogwood Dr, Conyers, GA 30208.

Straw Hat Cooperative: 6400 Village Pkwy, Dublin, CA 94568.

Subway Sandwiches and Salads: 25 High St, Milford, CT 06460.

Greeting Service

Dial-A-Gift, Inc.: 2265 E 4800 S, Salt Lake City, UT 84117.

Sonmark, Inc.: 130 Quigley Blvd, New Castle, DE 19720.

Stork News of America, Inc.: 6537 Raeford Rd, Ste 104, Fayetteville, NC 28404.

Health Aids & Services

Alpha Nurses of America: 2812 Buchanan, Wichita Falls, TX 76308.

American Medical Weight Association (N & J Medical Corp.): 1735 Merriman Rd, Akron, OH 44313.

America's Doctors Of Optometry, Inc.: 200 South St, Tracy, MN 56175.

Bodycues (The Elizabeth Corp.): 601 Moses Blvd, Dayton, OH 45408.

Cardiac Fitness Profile (Medical Plus Personal Fitness Profile, National Health Enhancement Systems): 3200 N Central, Ste 1750, Phoenix, AZ 85012.

Comp-u-med Systems, Inc.: 8549 Higuera St, Culver City, CA 90230.

Dermaculture Clinic: 1936 W 135th St, Gardena, CA 90249.

Eurotan International: 3701 Montrose Blvd, Houston, TX 77006.

Fortunate Life Weight Loss: 1600 Quail Run, Charlottesville, VA 22901.

Health Force: 160 Stewart, Hempstead, NY 11590.

Health Med Systems: 19337 NW 2nd Ave, Miami, FL 33169.

Oxygen Therapy Institute, Inc.: 21355 Hatcher Ave, Ferndale, MI 48220.

Professional Way Corp.: 27173 Grand River, Detroit, MI 48240.

Stop Smoking Plan: PO Box 232, E Amherst, NY 14051.

Laundry & Dry Cleaning

Duds 'N Suds: 3401 101st St, Des Moines, IA 50322.

King Koin, Inc.: 6900 E Camelback, Ste 700, Scottsdale, AZ 85251.

London Equipment Company: 2243 Bryn Mawr Ave, Philadelphia, PA 19131.

Motels, Hotels and Campgrounds

Brutger Hospitality Group: Box 399, St. Cloud, MN 56302.

Ramada Inns, Inc.: 3838 E Van Buren, Phoenix, AZ 85008.

Super 8 Motels: 1910 8th Ave NE, Aberdeen, SD 57401.

Pet Products and Services

Petland, Inc.: 195 N Hickory St, PO Box 1606, Chillicothe, OH 45601.

Pet Nanny of America: 1000 Long Blvd, Lansing, MI 48911.

Photography, Framing & Art

Frame & Save (Frame King, Inc.): 3126 Dixie Hwy, Erlanger, KY 41018.

Frame It Yourself: 55 W Main St, Ramsey, NJ 07466.

Nationwide Studios, Inc. (Teddy Bear Portraits): 400 N Belvedere Dr, Gallatin, TN 37066.

Pose With The President (Pose With The Stars, Innovative Ideas, Inc.): 3034 M St, Ste 200, Washington, DC 20007.

The Sports Section Photography, Inc.: 4958 Hammermill Rd, Atlanta, GA 30084.

Printing and Copying Services

American Speedy Printing Centers, Inc.: 2555 Telegraph, Bloomfield Hills, MI 48013.

Kwik-Kopy Printing Centers: One Kwik-Kopy Lane, Cypress, TX 77429.

Sir Speedy Printing: 23131 Verdugo Dr, Laguna Hills, CA 92653.

Real Estate

Century 21: 2601 SE Main St, Irvine, CA 92714.

Gallery of Homes: PO Box 2900, Orlando, FL 32812.

Realty World Corp.: 12500 Fair Lakes Cir, Ste 300.

RE/Max International, Inc.: PO Box 3907, Englewood, CO 80155.

Rental Services

A to Z Rental Centers, Inc.: 3550 Cedar Ave S, Minneapolis, MN 55407.

Formal Wear Service: 639 VFW Pkwy, Westbrook Hancock Village, Rte 1, Chestnut Hill, MA 02167.

Retail

Accentuate (Project Multiplication Int'l, Inc.): 12239 SW 132nd Ct, Miami, FL 33186.

Agway, Inc.: PO Box 4933, Syracuse, NY 13221.

Almost Heaven Hot Tubs Ltd.: Rt 5-I, Renick, WV 24966.

Annie's Book Stop: 15 Lackey St, Westborough, MA 01581.

Book Rack: 2703 E Commercial Blvd, Fort Lauderdale, FL 33308.

Decorating Den Systems, Inc.: 4630 Montgomery Ave, Bethesda, MD 20814.

Georgette Designs: 165½ Lower Via Casitas, Greenbrae, CA 94904.

Just Baskets International, Inc.: 1239 E Newport Center Dr, Ste 115, Deerfield Beach, FL 33442.

Light Bulbs Unlimited: 1203 Westheimer, Houston, TX 77002.

Mr Locksmithy Convenience Centre: 1828 Tribute Rd, Ste M Rear, Sacramento, CA 95815.

Network Video, Inc.: 5562 Quail Run N, Olmstead, OH 44070.

Re-Sell-It Shops, Inc.: 3316 Governor Dr, San Diego, CA 92122.

Silk Plants, Etc.: 1755 Butterfield Rd, Libertyville, IL 60048.

Sport It: 395 94th Ave NW, Coon Rapids, MN 55433.

Supernutrition: 531 44th Ave, San Francisco, CA 94121.

Take It Personal (International Gifts of Distinction, Inc.):
252 Kings Way, Naples, FL 33942.

Weather Or Not Parasols: 4747 Nob Hill Rd, Sunrise, FL 33321.

Wild Birds Unlimited: 1430 Broad Ripple Ave, Indianapolis, IN
46220.

WildTops: 600 Worcester Rd, Farmingham, MA 01701.

Retail: Computer, Electronics & Video

Home Call Mobile Video Libraries (MVL, Empire Enterprises, Inc.):
8233-10 Gator Lane, West Palm Beach, FL 33411.

Premiere Video Transfer: 215 Ellis Ave, Maryville, TN 37801.

Vidtron Drive Through Movie Rentals: PO Box 685, Granbury, TX
76048.

Schools

Alphabetland Pre-School Centers: 6 Passaic St, Hackensack, NJ
07601.

Educational Resource Centers of America, Inc.: Ste 202, 7000
Paletto Park Rd W, Boca Raton, FL 33433.

Mundus Institute Of Travel: PO Box 9800, Phoenix, AZ 85068.

SMI International, Inc.: 1600 Lake Air Dr, Waco, TX 76710.

The Travel Grade School: 609 W Littleton Blvd, Littleton, CO 80120.

USA Travel School, Inc.: 260 Sunny Isles Blvd, North Miami
Beach, FL 33160.

Sports & Recreation

Golfmat Corp.: 866 N Henry St, Alexandria, VA 22314.

Lomma Championship Miniature Golf Courses: 1120 S Washington Ave, Scranton, PA 18505.

Travel

Cruise Shoppes America Ltd.: 5100 Poplar, Ste 1219, Memphis, TN 38137.

Empress Travel Franchise Corp.: 450 Harmon Meadow Blvd, Secacus, NJ 07096.

Ports-O-Call Cruises, Inc.: 3501 N Causeway, Ste 103, Metairie, LA 70002.

Travel Agents International, Inc.: 111 2nd Ave, St Petersburg, FL 33731.

Miscellaneous

Air Brook Limousine: 115 W Passaic St, Rochester Park, NJ 07662.

Bavarian Wax Art: 6380 Euclid Rd, Cincinnati, OH 45236.

Control Data Corp. (Agricultural Products & Computer Services): PO Box 0, Minneapolis, MN 55440.

Create-A-Book: 6380 Euclid Rd, Cincinnati, OH 46236.

Legacy One, Inc.: 300 N Kanawha St, Box C, Beckley, WV 25801.

Meistergram: 3517 W Wendover Ave, Greensborough, NC 27402.

Monograms Today (Monograms America, Inc.): 5100 Westheimer, Ste 275, Houston, TX 77056.

Newspaper Headlines (Personally Yours): 6 Derby Rd, Hicksville, NY 11801.

Sound Tracks Recording Studios, Inc.: 424 Parkway, PO Box 329, Sevierville, TN 37862.

Tote-A-Shower, Inc.: Route 1, Box 172, Toledo, IL 62468.

Worldwide Refinishing Systems/GNU: 580 Lake Air Dr, Waco, TX 76710.

CHAPTER 8

The World of Mail Order

Mail order is one of the fastest growing and most lucrative areas of business today. It's usually easier to start a mail-order business because you can work from your home with a relatively small investment. It is also a business that can be successfully managed if you have another job.

Even so, you must understand that the same planning, research and development are required for mail order as for any other small business. Toward that end, this chapter gives you a working overview of the mail-order business and, more important, some excellent sources of information with which you can develop a business plan to sell your product or service by mail.

Deciding What to Sell

Few businesses require as little up-front investment as mail order. And if you do a proper market test you will know almost immediately whether or not you have a winning product—just by tracking the responses you get.

The Standard Rate and Data Service lists the most successful mail-order items:
1. Books
2. Wearing apparel
3. Hobbies and crafts

"DON'T TELL ME WE'RE OUT OF STAMPS!"

  4. Housewares
  5. Agriculture products
  6. Automotive services
  7. Cosmetics
  8. Health and comfort items
  9. Foods
  10. Entertainment products
  11. Sports and outdoor equipment
  12. Greeting cards and stationery
  13. Devices and gadgets
  14. Collectors' items
  15. Childcare and nursery items

When choosing a mail-order business make sure you are not competing with local merchants or with national catalogs that offer the same product. *Uniqueness* is the key here. Your product should have appeal as a novelty or specialty. You should be able to purchase it at a price that will allow you to mark it up enough to cover all your costs and show a profit. Ideally, the product should generate repeat sales.

Bear in mind *why* people buy through mail order: to save money, to enjoy the convenience of shopping at home, and/or to buy an item they haven't seen or can't get in a retail outlet.

The most successful mail-order businesses depend almost totally on the effectiveness of their advertising. The copy should be written to appeal in the best possible way to the potential customer. Ron Hume, president of Hume Publishing Company of Toronto, Ontario, has developed a successful financial-planning home-study service. Hume market-tested each word of his advertising copy before finalizing it. Your prose must convince the prospective buyer that your service or product is unique and offered at an excellent price. You might well consider retaining a professional copywriter when designing your ad.

After you have your basic ad design you should research magazines, newspapers, and other publications; select your customers and develop mailing lists; and study other mail-order ads to see how they present their products. Many publications' advertising rates will be too expensive for you initially, so look for publications that offer direct marketing through small ads. Then make sure the ads you see are repeated, because that tells you they are successful.

Among the least expensive and best venues for the beginning mail-order entrepreneur are the classified advertising pages of national and regional newspapers and magazines. These ads don't require fancy artwork and you can use your responses to build an inquiry list for your mail-order item. Not every product or service can be sold through classified sections, but check the various publications to see what kinds of things are being marketed in them.

A successful classified ad has four key elements:

1. It attracts ATTENTION with a key one- or two-word headline such as "Best Buy" or "One of a Kind."

2. There is an implied or direct PROMISE that the item will "Save Energy" or "Delight Your Friends."

3. There is a call for ACTION to "Send $1" or "Write."

4. The return address has a KEY letter or word to identify which periodical generated the response.

There are three other sources of mail-order business: telephone (telemarketing), television (particularly cable TV), and radio. We recommend, however, that you research those areas only after you have successfully tapped the print media.

Other Mail-Order Essentials

Mailing lists are a key factor in the success of any mail-order business and lists covering specialized markets can often be purchased. For example, if your product offers a collar for pets, you need to develop a list of pet owners. If you are selling a fishing lure, you need to put together a list of fishermen. If you purchase a list from a company that sells them, make sure it's exactly what you want and that it's as current as possible.

The package you mail to prospective customers is also very important. Generally it comprises an outside envelope, a sales letter, brochure or flyer, a guarantee, an order blank, testimonials, and a self-addressed return envelope (this is *most* important). Many of these things can be combined on one sheet. But the package can be expensive, so it must be carefully designed to show off your product to its best advantage. This kind of complete package should be developed only after you have market-tested your product.

It is essential that you determine if your product will sell in the particular medium using the specific marketing method you have chosen. Don't spend big money on a product or service until you have a clear indication that there are buyers who want it. This is why keying your advertising is so important: It allows you to track where most of your responses are coming from so you can concentrate on that area.

The Cost of Doing Business

Sending anything by mail today is costly. It is therefore imperative that you set up a budget with the rate of return from each mailing in mind. If you can get a 10 percent return, you will be doing extremely well.

It is also important that you know all applicable state and federal regulations. There are many levels of bulk mailing permits you can purchase, and knowing which one is right for you will cut your postage costs considerably.

Mail order is a wonderful area for the fledgling entrepreneur. But you need to learn as much about it as possible before you start. Refer to the mail-order resource list at the end of this book. All of these are good primers on the business, but if you read only one make it William A. Cohen's *Building a Mail Order Business* (John Wiley & Sons, Inc., 1982).

CHAPTER 9

The Rural Business

Rural areas offer a fair share of advantages not found in the city.

There was a time when a family could live comfortably off a farm of no more than a couple of dozen acres. Today, however, it takes many hundreds—even thousands—of acres for a viable operation. Recent decades have found farm kids moving to the city and leaving the farming to the giant agribusinesses. In some cases their parents remain on their land in retirement. And some city people return to their roots, buying small farms where they can retire.

Individuals living in rural areas have several distinct assets if they want to establish a business. They have some land, and access to rural crafts, recipes, and other products that offer the charm of the country.

Country Roads

The L. L. Bean General Store capitalized on its rural setting via a mail-order catalog that touts location and the traditional values of good quality and integrity in selling specialized outdoor clothing. Customers buying through the catalog get the feeling they are shopping in an old-fashioned general store without leaving home.

Another way to take advantage of the rural theme, even if you don't have any land, is to seek out and market the products indigenous to the area or region. Many small businesses use the terms

"New England" or "Rocky Mountain" to sell jams and jellies, chocolates, crafts, etc.

It's also possible to use a small parcel of land to produce something to sell. Since a small acreage cannot compete with large commercial agricultural concerns, of course, the trick here is to specialize.

Wilton Jaffee has six acres near his home 7,500 feet above sea level in the Rocky Mountains. He wondered what he could grow organically at that altitude. A little research told him that potatoes had been grown in the area during the mining days. Jaffee then researched potato-growing in the Peruvian Andes, and eventually chose two types of Peruvian potatoes that would thrive on his land.

Ten years later the 75-year-old Jaffee runs the only mail-order business for organically grown, high-altitude seed potatoes in the world. He services customers in the mountains of Hawaii, in the frigid areas of Alaska, and all across the country. Every year he sells out his stock.

Organically grown products are in big demand these days, and the crops are best handled on a small scale. Other possibilities: flowers, gourds, elephant garlic, purple potatoes, alpine strawberries, Christmas trees, catfish, llamas, rare birds and rabbits. Most of these are too specialized for the big agribusinesses to deal with, but there is a continuing demand for them. *You* might be able to fill that demand.

A New England restaurateur says his 150-year-old inn is well known as a dinner house. His secret is that he buys much of his gourmet produce like baby vegetables and exotic greens from nearby farmers who want to make a little extra money. Word spread of his needs and he seldom has to search for providers.

Business Co-Ops

If you should decide to grow a specialty crop and find that you don't have enough land, talk to your neighbors. The idea of farming co-operatives is an old one that still works.

One farmer did just that. He grew statice (which is commonly used in fresh and dried floral arrangements). The plant is easy to grow since it is little more than a thistle. The demand for his statice became so great that he sold his crop on a future basis even before it was planted. He finally invited several neighbors to join him in the venture. Now they tend each other's crops while one or the other takes a vacation and the supply has grown while the labor involved has decreased. Each year's entire crop is still sold before it's even seeded.

A woman started selling greenware (unfired ceramics) to craft shops throughout her area. She invested in molds and worked in her barn. Eventually she hired high school students to help unmold and clean the pieces. Still the demand grew. Finally, she asked several of her friends who were interested in ceramics to help. Today's co-op venture is highly successful.

Truck-farming is another possibility. For this, the closer you are to a major urban area the better your profit margin. With the decline in freshness and quality of supermarket produce, roadside stands and farmers' markets are once again the rage they were 50 years ago. In fact, many major market chains are adding organically grown produce sections. Work with neighbors to create a highly successful business in this field.

Finding a Market

Marketing is as important to a successful rural business as to a city-based one. Jaffee, who grows potatoes in the Rocky Mountains, uses a short series of classified ads in only one magazine. There's a woman who sells her homemade jellies and preserves to local resort and restaurant gift shops. One man put a catfish pond on his five-acre parcel and sells the entire crop to a local restaurant.

A California farmer has a small grove of olive trees on his 20-acre farm. It's not enough to make a living by commercial standards, but he makes a handsome supplementary income by selling the crop to families who still want to home-cure their own olives.

Many businesses prosper primarily *because* of their country locations. Bed-and-breakfast inns and dude ranches sell little more than clear skies, open fields and rural charm. A dairy farming couple put an ad in the city paper inviting families to come spend a week doing the chores and sharing their old farm house, which has ample space since their four children are grown and gone. Not only have they supplemented their income, but they have made many new acquaintances who return each year for a taste of farm life.

One retired couple turned their small farm into a pumpkin patch. They plant pumpkins on their acreage and leave them in the field so families can come out, choose and pick their own pumpkins off the vine. Over the years they have added animated Halloween displays, which of course delight the customers' youngsters. The farm looks like a crowded country fair on October weekends. The project supplements the couple's income nicely—and they have a lot of fun with it.

Another retiree carves wooden toys out of scraps he gets from a nearby lumber mill and sells his wares on a circuit of craft fairs in Northern California and Oregon. Several weekends a year he loads up his goods and takes off to enjoy an expense-paid vacation.

If you don't want to grow things, sometimes you can forage a product. Well-formed pinecones are a valuable commodity to craft shops and florists. Wild herbs are always in demand. Cattails from a marsh are also salable. The owners of Celestial Seasonings in Boulder, Colorado, began their business by gathering wild herbs from the hillsides and putting them in their now-famous teas. Their business grew so large the company is now part of a major corporation.

A retired couple in the hill country of Oregon actually started a zoo on their farm. They collected animals from defunct circuses and the like, and now people come from all over the state to see llamas, rabbits, buffalo, a monkey, elephant and zebra running wild alongside horses, chickens, peacocks, guinea fowl and other predictable farm animals.

Many rural locations offer ideal settings for craft shops, antique stores and second-hand shops. Owners glean items from the surrounding areas and offer them to city folks who enjoy driving out to the country and buying these types of goods—from the source.

Finally, be aware that today's technology makes it possible to run almost any business from a rural area. Many people have opened consultancies of one kind or another and relay their work by computer, telephone, and fax machine. One individual evaluates executive-level job candidates for large corporations in the Boston area—from his farm in Northern California!

CHAPTER 10

Women in Business

Women are entering the business and professional world in ever-increasing numbers. It follows that more and more women are starting their own businesses. I have received letters from hundreds of homemakers who are hesitant about starting a business because they've spent the last 15 to 25 years raising their families.

The business of running a household is very possibly the most demanding there is. To be a successful homemaker one must be an effective manager, treasurer, accountant, child-care expert, nutritionist, psychologist, recreation coordinator, purchasing agent, teacher, fashion consultant, interior decorator, travel planner, chauffeur, craftsperson, chef, record keeper, counselor and much, much more. For many women it's just a matter of convincing themselves that their skills and abilities are more than adequate to pursue and organize a business. However, the most important factor is that the business chosen should be something the woman enjoys doing. Only then is the formula for success complete.

There are millions of successful women entrepreneurs in the United States. Each has her own story. Some went into business after their children were grown; others after divorce or the death of a spouse. Some wanted to supplement their incomes but didn't want to re-enter the full-time workforce. Some wanted to channel their creativity profitably.

One 70-year-old California woman who is an excellent typist and word-processor got tired of being turned down for jobs because

of her age. She invested in a computer and printer and now runs a thriving secretarial business from her home.

Another woman organized her own publishing company at the age of 63, tapping into her past experiences as a newspaper reporter and editor.

Tips for Working at Home

Coralee Kern built a business after she was divorced and left with two children to raise alone. She began with a home cleaning service that became so successful she went on to start a newsletter specifically for people who work from home, *Mind Your Own Business at Home* (2520 N Lincoln Ave, No. 60, Chicago, IL 60614). Some of her tips for women (or anyone) working at home:

• Plan your work and work your plan. Practice self-discipline, make a schedule and follow it.

• Set up an office/studio/workroom apart from the rest of the house so you can work uninterrupted.

• Get up, get dressed and "go to work" every day.

• Be professional and hire professionals. Get expert advice on taxes and business laws.

• Install a separate business phone; buy a good answering machine or hire a reputable answering service.

• Have a reliable backup person who can keep your business running in your absence.

• Keep in touch with your industry by joining a professional association and subscribing to financial publications and trade journals.

Just a few of the myriad businesses that can be run from the home: babysitting, employment services, dressmaking/tailoring, photo development, art and graphic design, messenger/delivery services, research surveys, real estate sales, insurance sales, freelance writing, hairstyling, upholstery, pet/plant care, catering, tutoring,

KEEP IN TOUCH WITH OTHERS
THROUGH PROFESSIONAL AND CIVIC GROUPS.

gardening services, machine repair, taxi services, laundering/ironing, beauty care, handicrafts, newsletter publication, mail order, catalogs, elder care.

Hobbies such as pottery, photography, woodworking, scrimshaw, stained glass, antique-collecting, knitting or other needlework, cake-decorating, candymaking, jewelry design, sculpture, painting, cooking and engraving, to name a few, all lend themselves nicely to home businesses.

Companies like Mary Kay, Tupperware, Avon, Amway and Stanley Products all offer small-start-up-investment opportunities for the home-based businessperson. Before undertaking any of these ventures, however, be very sure this is what you want. The home sales business is a very competitive one, but it can also be very lucrative.

Home-based businesses run by women have become so numerous there is a National Alliance of Businesswomen (PO Box 95, Norwood, NJ 07648). Women from all over the U.S. bring their ideas, resources and problems to this group.

CHAPTER 11

Buying an Existing Business

Another viable option for the aspiring entrepreneur is to buy an already existing business. Look in any major metropolitan newspaper and you will find dozens of offerings under the "Business Opportunities" category: pet shops, clothing stores, rent-a-car lots, candle shops, boutiques, food and catering services, home-based mail-order businesses, and many more. These are usually listed as profitable concerns located in excellent locations that are available for a small cash down payment. Sounds great; but as with any other business, investigation is the byword.

Make your background and experience work for you when looking at an existing business. Don't buy one unless you have firsthand knowledge of and/or experience with its product or service. It's always best to go into something that is related to one of your former careers. For example, a football coach bought a fitness center, a travel agent bought a tour-bus company, and a chef bought a catering business. They, of course, had excellent prospects for success because they were familiar with the fields they entered.

Buyer Beware

Some vital points to cover in your investigation before taking over a business:

- Why is the business being sold? There are many valid

KICK THE TIRES FIRST!

justifications for selling a successful business: ill health, loss of interest, or retirement, for example. But if the reasons include new competition in the area, bad operating practices, etc., be careful.

•   What is the market condition in the area, both for the present and for future growth opportunities? Research this carefully.

•   What is the competition in the area? Check it out.

•   What is the reputation in the community of both the company and the current owner? Ask other businesspeople as well as individuals.

•   What are the credit status and business history? Check with a credit bureau and the local chamber of commerce.

•   How financially solid is the business? Have a competent accountant review its balance sheets and tax returns for the last five years and give you a net-worth figure.

•   How does the company stand legally? Have a small-business attorney review mortgages on property and equipment, leases, rights-of-way and easements, financing agreements, insurance, zoning and building-code regulations, copyrights, trademarks and name identification.

•   What is the real value of the goods and materials in stock? Be a hard negotiator here. No inventory is worth what the seller paid for it. Most should be sold at somewhere between 25 and 50 percent of the original cost. This includes office equipment as well as merchandise.

•   What is the business really worth? Look at such factors as profitability, rate of return on investment, expense ratio of the business, inventory, condition of the furnishings, fixtures and other property. Here again, consult professionals.

THE NUTS AND BOLTS

Business Facts Almanac

"Make no little plans;
they have no magic to stir men's blood."
—Daniel Hudson Burnham

The old saying "the race goes not to the swift but to the surefooted" has become a cliché precisely because it is so true. Those who plan well, look where they are going and step carefully will be the winners.

The system is the solution.
—AT&T

You should know now that a man of knowledge lives by act-
ing, not by thinking about acting, nor by thinking about what
he will think when he has finished acting. A man of knowledge
chooses a path with heart and follows it.
—Carlos Castaneda in *A Separate Reality*

This section contains worksheets to help you figure out exactly what type of business would best suit you, and to understand more clearly some of the nuts and bolts such as business types, management techniques, personnel needs, product analysis, location considerations, and competition assessment.

Forms of Doing Business

There are five primary forms of doing business that may be appropriate for you, and they are described briefly below. Seek competent tax and legal advice to complete the steps.

Step 1: Identify advantages and disadvantages of each form for the type of business you have in mind.

Sole Proprietorship
You alone own and operate the business. You own all assets and are entitled to all profits that may accrue, but you are also solely responsible for all debts and liabilities and must suffer the consequences of all losses that may result. It is extremely easy to start this type of business and there are no taxes other than your individual income tax.

Advantages and disadvantages of sole proprietorship:

_____

_____

_____

_____

General Partnership
You and at least one other person own and operate the business. You share the profits and losses, the assets and liabilities according to a written partnership agreement—recommended but not required — or an oral understanding. Partners pay income taxes on their individual shares of the profits, but no tax on the partnership.

Advantages and disadvantages of a general partnership:

_____

_____

_____

_____

Limited Partnership

This is similar to a general partnership, but there are two types of part-ners: general and limited. Limited partners are limited in legal liabil-ity to an amount based on their capital contributions to the business.

Advantages and disadvantages of a limited partnership:

_____

_____

_____

_____

Regular Corporation

A corporation is itself a legal entity you form alone or with other owners. It must have articles of incorporation or bylaws, and proper establishment generally requires a lawyer's expertise. A corporation does business in its own name, separate from you and the other owners. The owners' liability is limited to an amount based on their investment in stock. The corporation itself pays taxes, and owners must pay individual income taxes on any salaries and/or dividends they receive from the corporation.

Advantages and disadvantages of a regular corporation:

_____

_____

_____

_____

Chapter S Corporation

This is like a regular corporation in all legal aspects, but the owners are taxed like owners of a partnership.

Advantages and disadvantages of an S corporation:

_____

_____

_____

_____

Step 2: Determine the form of business you will use.

Selected form of doing business:

_____

_____

_____

_____

Management

Step 1: Identify owners and key employees.

a. What form of business have you selected?
b. Who are the owners and what are their titles?
c. Who are the key employees and what are their titles?
d. When have these people previously worked together?

Owners and key employees:

_____

_____

_____

_____

_____

_____

Step 2: Develop a résumé for each owner and key employee.

Each résumé should include the person's name and title and answer the following questions in order:
a. What are the person's important duties?
b. What is the person's previous business experience?
c. What is the person's educational background?

d. What are the person's personal interests?
e. Who are the person's references?

Owner and key employee résumés:

_____

_____

_____

_____

_____

_____

_____

_____

_____

Step 3: Identify outside consultants and advisers.

a. Who is your accountant?   _____

b. Who is your lawyer?   _____

c. Who is your banker?   _____

d. Who is your insurance broker?   _____

e. Who are your references?   _____

Outside consultants and advisers:

_____

_____

_____

Step 4: Complete the business skills matrix.

This exercise will help you identify areas of business expertise where you need to seek assistance. For each skill area, put an "I" in the adequate knowledge column to indicate that an insider (owner or key employee) has the skill, an "O" to indicate an outsider has the skill. For each area where you have not indicated adequate knowledge, put an "X" in either the assistance needed or education needed column.

Management Skills	Adequate Knowledge	Assistance Needed	Education Needed
Accounting & taxes	_____	_____	_____
Planning	_____	_____	_____
Organizing	_____	_____	_____
Financial management	_____	_____	_____
People management	_____	_____	_____
Time management	_____	_____	_____
Personal selling	_____	_____	_____
Promotion	_____	_____	_____
Decisionmaking	_____	_____	_____
Cost control	_____	_____	_____
Personnel policies	_____	_____	_____
Pricing	_____	_____	_____

Step 5: Determine how to address needed skill areas.

For each skill area marked with an "X," determine how you will satisfy the specific need.

To compensate for areas where management skill is still lacking:

_____

_____

_____

_____

_____

_____

_____

Personnel

Step 1: Identify needed employees.

a. *How many employees will you have?*
b. *What are the job titles for and skills needed by employees?*

Needed employees:

_____

_____

_____

_____

_____

Step 2: Identify source of employees.

Good employees can make the difference between a successful business and a marginal one. It is important to know where and how to find qualified employees for your particular type of business. It is also important to identify where your employees can receive training, whether on the job through a work-study program or from an outside source.

a. *How will you obtain needed employees?*
b. *What problems will you have finding competent employees?*
c. *What training is available in your community for your employees?*

Source of employees:

_____

_____

_____

_____

_____

_____

_____

_____

Step 3: Identify costs of employees.

The costs associated with having employees are much greater than the wages you pay; they are usually the biggest single on-going cost of running a business. There are costs that are required by law, as well as many optional ones.

a. What are the base wages or salaries?_____

b. What will be the cost of required employee benefits? _____

    Employer portion of Social Security?_____

    Employer portion of unemployment insurance? _____

    Workers' compensation insurance? _____

c. What will be the cost of optional employees benefits?_____

    Medical/dental insurance? _____

Life/disability insurance? _____

Pension/profit-sharing plan? _____

Cost of employees:

_____

_____

_____

_____

Step 4: Determine when to develop needed written policies.

Written job descriptions that clearly define the duties of each employee and a written personnel-policy manual that details the relationship between employee and employer are vital documents. (Hint: you may be able to borrow a manual from a going business and adapt it.)

a. When will you complete your written job descriptions?

_____

b. When will you complete a written personnel-policy manual?

_____

Written personnel policies:

_____

_____

_____

Products/Services

Step 1: Identify products offered for sale.

a. What product(s) will your business sell?
b. Who will be your key product suppliers?
c. What makes your product(s) unique?
d. Why will customers purchase products from you?

Product(s) offered for sale:

_____

_____

_____

_____

Step 2: Define the economics of the product(s) being sold.

a. What prices will be charged?
b. What costs are associated with the product(s)?
c. How profitable and competitive are the prices?
d. What levels of inventory will be required?

Economics of product(s) for sale:

_____

_____

_____

_____

Step 3: Identify service(s) offered for sale.

Unlike products, services do not generally carry a brand name for the customer to choose. Instead, the customer often chooses a service based on impressions of your business. Services are more abstract than products because there is nothing for the customer to see or feel. However, like products, your services must have some attributes that will make the customer want them.

a. *What service(s) will you provide?*
b. *What problems will the service(s) solve?*
c. *What makes the service(s) unique?*

Service(s) offered for sale:

_____

_____

_____

_____

_____

_____

_____

_____

Step 4: Define economics of services.

a. *What prices will be charged for the service(s)?*
b. *What costs will be associated with the service(s)?*
c. *Will the service(s) be profitable and competitively priced?*

Economics of service(s) offered for sale:

_____

_____

_____

_____

_____

_____

_____

_____

_____

Customers

Step 1: Describe your customer.

If your customers are other businesses, the following information may be useful in defining your typical customer.

Industry: _____

Annual sales volume: _____

Age of business: _____

If your customers are members of the general public, the following information may be helpful:

Marital status: _____   Sex: _____

Income level: _____   Age range: _____

Education: _____   Cultural background: _____

Activities, hobbies, special interests: _____

_____

Step 2: Determine location of customers.

a. What distance are customers willing to travel to buy from you?

_____

b. What distance will you travel to sell to your customers?

_____

Step 3: Determine number of potential customers.

This step will require some research. If selling to the general public, you need to look at some census data. (Check with your chamber of commerce or write to the Census Bureau.) If selling to other businesses, there are many potential sources of information, one of the best being a trade association. Check with your local Small Business Development Center office or visit your local library.

How many customers you described live within the geographical

limits you have determined for your business? _____

Step 4: Determine the number who will purchase from you.

For this tough step, you need to carefully consider your competition, both in numbers and quality (more on this on a later worksheet). You also need to realize that some of your potential customers will not patronize you OR a competitor.

a. *How many potential customers will buy the product(s) or service(s)*

   from either you or a competitor? _____

b. *What percentage of those who do make a purchase will choose*

   your business? _____

c. *Multiply a by b to determine the number of potential customers*

   who will purchase from your business. _____

Step 5: Determine average customer sales per year.

This will also require research. Trade associations or industry publications are good sources for the data needed here.

a. *How many purchases of your product(s) or service(s) will the average customer make in a year?* _____

b. *How much will the average customer spend for each purchase he or she makes?*_____

c. *Multiply a by b to determine the amount an average customer will spend each year.* _____

Step 6: Determine your annual sales volume.

You know the number of customers and the average amount each customer will spend in a year. Multiply these two figures to calculate your expected annual sales volume.

_____

Step 7: Evaluate the annual sales volume figure.

Does the figure in step 6 make sense to you? (Use your intuition.) If not, go back to step 3 and try again. Be careful not to indulge in wishful thinking; look at this with a hard eye.

Location

Step 1: Describe the location of your business.

a. *What is the address of your business?*
b. *What features make this a good location for your business?*
c. *What nearby businesses will help you attract customers?*

Location of business:

_____

_____

_____

_____

Step 2: Describe future needs of your location.

a. *What are the physical features of your building?*
b. *What are the appearances of nearby buildings?*

Appearance of business:

_____

_____

_____

_____

Step 3: Determine future needs and
identify occupancy costs of your location.

a. *What renovations will be needed, and what will they cost?*
b. *What are the prospects for business growth in the area?*
c. *What are the terms of lease or purchase for your location?*
d. *What are the annual costs of your location?*

Future prospects of the location:

Annual occupancy costs: _____

Rent or mortgage payments: _____

Property taxes: _____

Maintenance and repairs: _____

Insurance: _____

Utilities: _____

Other costs: _____

TOTAL ANNUAL COSTS: _____

TOTAL COSTS PER SQUARE FOOT: _____

Step 5: Prepare visual aids to show location to outsiders.

Location is an extremely important factor in whatever type of business you have in mind (unless you are using your home or planning to work only through mail order). For most retail and many small service businesses, location can be critical to your success. For retail and service businesses, customer access and visibility are vital. For wholesale and manufacturing businesses, access to resources—labor, materials, transportation and utilities—is essential. It is often best to identify your location for an outsider with maps, pictures, and a diagram of the layout. (Even if you plan to use your home, a diagram of how you will arrange the work area is of interest to those who may decide to finance you.)

Take pictures of your business and the surrounding businesses.

On a map of the area, indicate the location of your business and any major reference points.

Draw an accurate diagram of your floor space, showing the locations of equipment, furniture and fixtures. (If you have no idea where to place equipment and fixtures most effectively, visit businesses similar to yours to get some ideas.)

Step 6: Obtain copies of legal documents.

Have readily available a copy of the lease or purchase agreement and any other legal documents that may affect your ability to use the location for your business. (Just because the previous owner used a neighboring driveway for deliveries, for example, does not mean the same service will extend, legally, to your business. Investigate carefully to make sure.)

Competitive Analysis

A key to business success is establishing a unique market niche. In this section you must carefully compare your business with four major competitors. (If there are not four in your immediate area, look beyond it for competitors who may be planning to move into your market.) Use the forms on these pages to record the ranking of your competitors. Be objective and honest with yourself—the purpose is to help you to identify where you have a competitive advantage, as well as where you need to improve.

Step 1: Identify your competition.

Names and addresses of four major competitors:

1. _____

2. _____

3. _____

4. _____

Step 2: Compare your business to the competition.

Compare your business with your competitors in each of the following:
a. Image—This includes both the physical appearance of the business and its reputation in the community.
b. Location—How convenient is the location? Key considerations are distance from customers, traffic access, parking and visibility.

c. Layout—Consider the physical layout, especially as it relates to serving customers.

d. Atmosphere—Is the feeling a customer has in the place of business suitable for the type of business?

e. Product(s)—How complete are product lines, and are there name brands in stock?

f. Service(s)—Look at both quantity and quality.

g. Pricing—This may be difficult to compare, but assume that the lowest price is most attractive to customers if all else is equal.

h. Advertising—Are the media being used reaching the target market?

i. Sales method—What selling techniques are used once customers are at the place of business?

Now rank yourself and each of your four competitors on a scale of 1 (lowest) to 5 (highest):

Areas of Comparison	You	Competitor			
		1	2	3	4
a. Image	___	___	___	___	___
b. Location	___	___	___	___	___
c. Layout	___	___	___	___	___
d. Atmosphere	___	___	___	___	___
e. Product(s)	___	___	___	___	___
f. Service(s)	___	___	___	___	___
g. Pricing	___	___	___	___	___
h. Advertising	___	___	___	___	___
i. Sales method	___	___	___	___	___

Step 3: Identify changes to improve your competitive position.

List changes that will improve your competitive position:

_____

_____

_____

_____

_____

_____

CHAPTER 12

Financing Your Business

A major ingredient in any successful business is proper planning for and projection of financial needs. It is therefore crucial to determine exactly how much you can personally afford to invest, how much collatoral you can risk, and how much outside money you can generate.

You also need to establish a sound banking relationship—and more than financing is involved in that. You will need at least one checking account for the business. If you sell merchandise you will need a merchant's account so you can offer credit-card charging to your customers. (In fact, many service providers also offer this convenience.) And you will probably need some sort of financing from the bank.

Shopping for the right bank is at least as important as shopping for anything else—perhaps more important, says Sherman Andelson, chairman of the board of The Bank of Los Angeles. "Start with the bank where you are already known, then branch out. Ask friends and business acquaintances about their banks, then mention to the loan officer that you were referred by so-and-so when you introduce yourself." Go into a bank with complete confidence. Don't be intimidated: You are the customer, after all. Don't do business with a bank that doesn't make you feel important.

And don't let a refusal discourage you. Not all banks put their emphases on the same things. You could be turned down by Bank A

"I WAS HOPING YOU MIGHT HAVE A SPECIAL ON GRANDCHILDREN!"

and welcomed with open arms by Bank B simply because the latter is more interested in making business loans than the former. "The bank loan officer will probably be your best and cheapest source of good advice," adds Andelson.

Keep in mind that a bank is not interested in taking risks; it will make sure it is covered for any eventuality. *You* are the risk-taker in your business venture. "Banks look first at your cash flow," says Andelson. "From this they determine how much available cash you have to meet your obligations. Next they look at your collateral." But different banks have different criteria, so if one refuses you a loan, go on to another—and another if necessary.

Further, do you know about the Small Business Administration?

Every year the SBA is alloted money by Congress to back loans to small businesses. Because the SBA guarantees loans for up to 90 percent, banks generally make them at an excellent interest rate. To find out the requirements write Small Business Administration, 1441 L St NW, Washington, DC 20416.

Be prepared to give the bank a complete and professional proposal of your business intentions. Know in advance the level of financing you will need, what you can afford to invest of your own resources, and how much you can afford to repay in regular installments.

Because you're an older person, be prepared for the bank to require term insurance on your loan. This because it doesn't want to have to deal with an estate and all the problems that would entail should you die before the loan is repaid.

No older person should gamble his or her life savings on a business venture. Keep in mind that at least half of all new businesses fail in the first year, and invest only an amount you could—worst case—lose in toto without being left destitute. Even with the help of this book, which should raise your chances of success well above the norm, you must do a great deal of research, planning, legwork and funding development before deciding to go into business.

DON'T BORROW SO MUCH THAT IT KEEPS YOU AWAKE AT NIGHT!

Test Your Credit Worthiness

You have a better chance of succeeding in business than younger people because of your experience, maturity and stability. You have had plenty of time to establish good credit.

Just to give yourself an idea of your credit-worthiness, go over the following six C's of credit:

1. Character and stability. You undoubtedly have a long list of character references—a most important consideration when raising capital.

2. Capability. The experience gained during your previous career will be a definite plus when you seek additional money for your business venture.

3. Capital. You should have a decent personal nest egg by now, and it is important that you invest some of your own capital in your business. This shows that you have enough confidence in your idea to take a personal risk.

4. Collateral. Chances are you have accumulated quite a bit of personal collateral—a home, paid-up insurance policies, etc.—that you can pledge to obtain a business loan.

5. Community competitiveness. You will be prepared to show the funding institution your extensive research concerning your product's or service's chance for success in the area where you want to start your business.

6. Coverage. If you already have—or have concrete plans to obtain—life, business-interruption, liability and fire insurance, the lending institution will be more willing to work with you.

Putting It All Together

Now that you've checked your credit potential, the next step is to put together a package that will tell a prospective lender your story. This package should contain the following:

- A recent personal financial statement.
- A booklet or brochure explaining your business.
- Sample ads and/or customer lists.
- A market research report.
- Sales projections based on careful market research.
- A cash-flow projection for your business.
- Any available articles about you or your business.

Financial Resources

Banks and other traditional lending institutions are much more willing to loan money for the expansion of an existing business than for the creation of a new one. So be prepared to tap other sources for your start-up costs. Some possible alternatives:

- **Personal savings.** Never risk more of your personal funds than you can afford to lose. If your business should fail, you will still need to take care of day-to-day living expenses as well as have money for retirement, emergencies, etc.
- **Retirement funds.** You may have built up an IRA; or you may have worked for a company that offered profit-sharing or a lump-sum retirement payment. Any of these can be used to help start your business. If you currently belong to a credit union, you might obtain a loan at a lower interest rate.
- **Personal collateral.** You have probably paid off your home mortgage and may have certificates of deposit or other securities. Any of these can be used for a loan. But remember, the loan should be small enough that you could make the payments out of your pension or other income should your business fail.
- **Venture capital.** This is the most difficult method of raising money. Venture capitalists are very, very savvy businesspeople who won't invest in anything that is not almost a sure thing. If you have what *they* consider a really great idea for a new business,

chances are they would be interested in investing in it. Realize, however, that you will probably lose a lot of control over your business if you go this route.

• **Friends and relatives.** There are countless wealthy individuals in this country who are not venture capitalists but who have both the resources and the desire to back a promising business endeavor. Do you know anyone in this category? Also, think about asking friends and/or relatives for a loan; if your business proposition is attractive, they may go along with you. Just enter such an arrangement with extreme caution: Would it be worth risking the loss of a treasured personal relationship if things went sour?

• **Suppliers.** An important financial resource can be your product suppliers, and your terms-of-payment negotiations with them are all-important. For instance, if you can negotiate a 60- or 90-day delay of payment for your inventory, it will probably reduce the amount of start-up capital you need to borrow.

It *is* possible to start a business on a shoestring. Daddy Bruce is a perfect example of an entrepreneur who made it big against all odds. And he did it by borrowing a small amount without risking his life savings (which were miniscule anyway).

Daddy Bruce—real name Bruce Randolph—is a Southern farmer/preacher's son with only a third-grade education. He learned his only skills from his grandmother, who was also the one who gave him her recipe for barbecue pork-roll, ribs and chicken. In 1959 he arrived in Denver, Colorado, flat broke. He worked for a year and managed to get a loan from an Englewood bank to buy a tiny, sad-looking barbecue pit. Thus was born Daddy Bruce's Barbecued Ribs. Today, at 70, Randolph runs a 200-person-capacity restaurant and employs a dozen people. Business is great.

CHAPTER 13

Choosing an Accountant

The Roman poet Horace wrote that money either serves or governs those who have it. To make your money serve you in business you have to know where it is going and where it is coming from. This itself can take up so much of your time that you may not be able to run your business properly. Many people start out thinking they can forgo the services of a professional accountant. It is the biggest mistake they can make.

A good accountant is worth his/her weight in gold—literally. He/she not only will keep the records that are required by law, but will also keep your business on track financially and give you guidelines to help you make decisions for the future.

Shop around for a good accountant. Ask friends and business acquaintances. Find an accountant who is interested in you, and he/she will be among your most valuable allies in starting and maintaining a successful business.

Setting Up the Books

Setting up an accounting system is a complex task. There are tax (income, sales, employee, etc.) liabilities to be determined. Journals and ledgers must be set up and divided into categories. A bank account must be established for business receipts and a petty cash

"OH I KNOW THOSE RECEIPTS ARE IN HERE . . . !"

fund for incidentals. A business-expense tracking system must be initiated. A filing system must be set up and maintained for checks, deposit slips, accounts payable, sales slips, invoices, canceled checks, etc. And all this is just to get started.

As you proceed into business and hire employees you will have to keep track of federal and state income tax withheld, Social Security and Medicare payments, unemployment and workers' compensation insurance premiums, and state and local taxes. Then there are federal and state tax returns, sales taxes, property taxes and business license fees to contend with. Obviously an accountant is essential from day one of planning your new business.

This is not to say you hire an accountant and have him/her take complete control of the books. You should have more than a working knowledge of basic accounting so you can review records and work with your accountant through all the business processes. One excellent book you could find useful is *Practical Accounting for a Small Business* by Lynn and Laura Taetzsch (Petrocelli/Charter, Princeton, NJ 08540).

CHAPTER 14

Name That Business

Choosing a name for your business is a very important step—and one that might not be as simple as you think. Too often a small business spends money on a name that turns out to be already in use. The business then has to change its name or face a lawsuit.

Thus it is important to do a search with an attorney specializing in patents/trademarks/copyrights when you decide upon a name. If you find that the name isn't already in use, have the attorney register it so you won't run into problems down the road. Registering a name ensures that no one else will use it. If your business is a proprietorship, register its name at the county court house; a corporation's name should be registered with the secretary of state. Laws vary, so check out registration requirements in your area.

One example of the importance of a name check involved an individual who decided to ship his imported pineapples under the company name Acapulco Gold. Before he went to the expense of buying licenses and permits and having promotional material, shipping crates, stationery, etc. printed, he wisely had an attorney run a check. The findings: no fewer than 26 firms named Acapulco Gold—including one that shipped pineapples.

Another caveat when choosing a name is to research its meanings and connotations, especially if it includes any foreign words. You want a name that is descriptive, clever and easy to remember. Bear in mind that its name will be each prospective customer's first contact with your business.

"LISTEN, BUSTER, MY NAME IS MOM. TAKE IT OR LEAVE IT!"

If you pick a generic or nondescriptive name, its advertising value may be nil and you will expend more effort conveying what your business sells than how good your product or service is. No one would know that a Big Mac is a hamburger without the millions of dollars McDonalds spent promoting it. But if your business is called Joe's Hamburgers, everyone will know what you sell.

Licenses and Permits

Almost every type of business requires a license or permit to operate. Find out what your city, county and state require. Even if you operate out of your home you must be sure you are conforming to zoning laws and have the proper license. Ask your accountant and your local business bureau or chamber of commerce where to check on what you need. Much depends on your business: For example, if you want to operate an ambulance you go to the board of health for a license; to open a day-care center you go to the department of social services.

Don't take any chances. Virtually every business you can think of requires some sort of license, so contact your city's business licensing department; its representative can tell you what licenses and permits you need to operate legitimately.

Trademarks

Trademarks are registered with the United States Patent and Trademark office in Washington, D.C. A trademark is defined as ''any word, name, symbol, or device, or a combination thereof adopted and used by a manufacturer or merchant to identify his goods and distinguish them from those manufactured or sold by others.'' The right to trademark is acquired only by use; registration is recognition by the government of the owner's right to use the mark.

RESEARCH FIRST TO FIND OUT IF IT'S BEEN DONE BEFORE.

A trademark has to be used in commercial sales. It will not be trademarked if it is similar to existing marks or copies a United States, state or local insignia, uses a celebrity's name, etc. In seeking a trademark for your goods, seek out an attorney in this field who will first make a search and then process the application for you. Your application will have to be submitted with a drawing, five specimens or facsimiles of the product, and the patent fee. This somewhat complicated process is best handled by a professional— but find out what his/her fee will be; the services involved can be quite costly.

Copyrights

A copyright is the exclusive legal right to reproduce, publish or sell the matter and form of a literary, musical or artistic work. Such things as art, books, articles, musical compositions, photographs, prints, drawings, sculptures and paintings fall under the copyright law.

If you have an item you feel may be in the copyright category, check by writing to the Copyright Office, Library of Congress, 10 First St SE, Washington, DC 20540. You can also request a copy of the copyright law and an application for the registration of a claim to copyright.

Why is a copyright important to you? If a publisher wants to buy your book, for example, he will buy the copyright and it protects him as sole publisher of the work. He is in effect paying you for the copyright. A copyright is most important when dealing with artistic commodities.

As in trademarking, it is recommended that you enlist the help of an attorney. In general, however, if you are sending a manuscript, photo or whatever to a reputable publisher there is little need to copyright the work first.

One trick writers use to establish an unofficial copyright is to put a copy of their manuscript in a sealed envelope and send it to themselves by registered mail. When it arrives it is dated and signed for. The *unopened* envelope is then put away for safekeeping. If the writer should find later that any part of his/her manuscript or story idea has been stolen, the unopened registered envelope will be admitted by the court as evidence of prior ownership.

CHAPTER 15

The Importance of Insurance

Business insurance is so important it should automatically be figured in as part of you start-up costs. Planning for it begins with an assessment of the kinds of risks you will be facing in your new venture. Generally, the following risks are covered by business insurance:

- Business interruption due to damage to the firm's assets.
- Personal injury to customers, employees or the public.
- Death or disability of key employees that results in a loss of business.
- Loss of or damage to the firm's property (supplies, fixtures, building, etc.).

Many businesses have failed because their owners were unaware there was such a thing as business-interruption insurance. A standard fire policy covers only losses due to fire; business-interruption insurance takes care of consequential losses of many types, including:

- Loss of building.
- Continuing post-fire expenses such as salaries, advance rent payments and interest obligations.
- The cost of temporary headquarters.
- Loss of rental income on buildings damaged or destroyed by fire if you are the landlord.

Another type of insurance no business should be without is general liability. This combined with vehicle liability (if appropriate) and standard workers' compensation should give you adequate

"NO THANKS. I'M COVERED!"

coverage. Again, a reputable insurance agent is your best source of information. He/she will design a package that best fits your needs *and* pocketbook. Again, however, shop around and compare premiums for the various kinds of insurance.

Coverages to discuss with your agent:

- Fire and general property damage (due to fire, vandalism, hail, wind, etc.).
- Plate-glass breakage.
- Burglary.
- Fraud (bad checks, larceny, counterfeit currency, etc.).
- Public liability.
- Workers' compensation (for on-the-job injuries).
- Key-man insurance (on the employer/owner's life).
- Partnership insurance (on the partners' lives).
- Fidelity bonding (covers theft by employees).

Appropriate insurance coverage is not static. As your income goes up and your business grows, it is important to review and adjust your coverages accordingly.

CHAPTER 16

Choosing the Legal Form of Your Business

A sole proprietorship is an enterprise owned by a single individual—no partners of any kind. This is the easiest form for a beginning business. The only requirements are that the name be filed with the county clerk and a business license be purchased. Drawback: Creditors can go after you personally and attach your property and bank accounts; this could reflect negatively on your personal credit rating since the credit history of the business is registered as your own personal credit.

A partnership is a popular legal form of business because partners can pool resources, skills and time. Drawbacks: The partners have unlimited liability and each is responsible for the acts of the other(s).

A corporation is often considered the best kind of business structure. It is itself a legal entity without reference to particular individuals who share in its ownership and/or direct its activities, so has the advantage of limiting the legal and financial liabilities of its stockholders. A corporation continues to exist after the death of the owners, and ownership is easily transferred. Drawback (particularly for a small business): The corporate profits and losses stay within the corporation.

A Chapter S. corporation is a less well known but sensible alternative, especially for companies with fewer than 35 stockholders. A Chapter S corporation shares the advantages of a regular corporation; but *unlike* a regular corporation, it can pass its

"DON'T SUE ME—SUE THE COMPANY!"

profits and losses directly to the income statements of its stock-holders. It is a form of business that is relatively simple and inex-pensive to set up. More important, start-up costs can be deducted from your personal income taxes, which is not the case with a regu-lar corporation. Chapter S. corporations also offer some excellent tax advantages. Ask your accountant and attorney about this option.

CHAPTER 17

Marketing and Advertising

Setting up a viable and effective marketing strategy early is essential to your success. Like every other facet of your business, effective marketing of your product/service takes basic planning and research. This should focus on the needs and desires of the consumer—your prospective customer. You must be totally dedicated to giving satisfaction to your customers and to building confidence in your product/service among them.

One advantage of a small business is that you can know your customers better and serve them more effectively. You can also often reach your smaller segment of the consumer public more quickly, thus saving advertising dollars.

To decide where you and your business fit into the market, ask yourself the following questions:

- Who are my customers?
- How many customers should I pursue?
- Where will I find my customers?
- Are there other products/services in my market area that are similar to mine?
- Am I offering something customers can't get anywhere else?
- How can I convince potential customers to do business with me?
- Have I researched my market well enough to answer the above questions?

The importance of correctly assessing your prospective customers' needs and wants cannot be overemphasized. And this important step can only be completed by setting up a viable marketing plan.

If you have a good marketing plan before you start your business, everything else will fall into place. The plan will be valuable in helping you obtain financing, hire competent personnel, and identify your prime customers. It will also help you utilize your resources most advantageously. It is obviously important to develop a plan that will sell your product/service not only to yourself but to prospective employees, financial backers, suppliers and customers. A good format for a formal marketing plan follows.

Title of Plan

Contents
- Background/Objectives—a business description.
- Product/Service description.
- Management credentials.
- Market potential (competition analysis).
- Market strategy for growth.
- Financial requirements.
- Summary of business venture, its merits, and why it will succeed.

Mapping Your Market

Too often a prospective small-business owner dismisses this step as "too time consuming" or "too expensive." But a proper market assessment doesn't have to be expensive. And if you are going to

TAKE YOUR PRODUCT TO THE CUSTOMER WHO NEEDS IT.

take a financial risk, it is essential to show backers you understand and know your market and that you have a plan to most effectively sell your product or service.

Victor Lowe, president of the Cool Car Corporation, is an excellent example of a small-business owner who used creative planning to develop a new product and find, test and expand his markets. On a visit to Israel, Lowe discovered a cardboard sunscreen die-cut to fit into an automobile windshield. He thought it might be successfully marketed in the United States. Before he launched the new product he tested it and found that it did indeed keep a car's interior 30 percent cooler as well as prevent sun damage to the dashboard. After additional testing he introduced the sunscreen; he sold 40,000 units the first month, $2 million worth the first year.

Lowe's success was no accident. It was the result of a well-thought out plan:

1. He tested his product to evaluate its performance.

2. He tested it on potential customers through the use of focus groups, which allowed him to see reactions first hand. It was then he decided not to distribute the sunscreen through car manufacturers, but to offer it directly to the public.

3. He tested it in the geographic areas where he thought it would get the most use: Southern California and Phoenix, Arizona.

4. He took the sunscreen to several large auto-parts stores and initially met with resistance. "That's only a piece of cardboard," they said. But because he had his market research results in hand, he was able to convince them that despite its simplicity, it was a potentially successful product.

5. He developed a comprehensive business plan that included a clear understanding of cash flow so he could support needed advertising and promotion.

6. He hired professionals early on to counsel him all along the way.

Ron Poppiel updated an idea for a potato peeler he saw sold at state fairs and, using the same sales pitch on television, sold millions of dollars' worth of Vegematics. This and other products made Poppiel a millionaire many times over.

No matter how innovative your product is, you need a marketing plan that includes the four P's:

1. Product. It's not hard to come up with an idea for a product or service. Look around you; draw on your creativity and experience. You can devise a completely new concept or build on and improve an old one.

2. Price. You can price your product/service high, low, or to match the competition. A low price is used to break into the market, but be careful: You don't want the consumer to infer that your product is inferior or cheap in any way. Most new companies set their prices in line with the competition's. If you do that, be prepared to convince prospective customers that you are offering a better value.

3. Place. Knowing where you are going to distribute your product is very important. No single channel can be used for all products or services. As a small-business person be aware that certain distribution channels are more effective than others in terms of cost and efficiency. Initially, Victor Lowe thought about distributing his sunscreen to auto manufacturers. Ron Poppiel is convinced he would never have been as successful as he was had he not chosen to market his products on television.

4. Promotion. Advertising and sales campaigns must be planned and carried out throughout the life of your business. This because you must keep the product or service fresh and viable in the mind of the consumer.

Plotting Your Advertising

You will need to spend as much as 5 percent of your total volume on advertising. During your first year of operation, in fact, and depending on your product's markup, you may have to budget up to

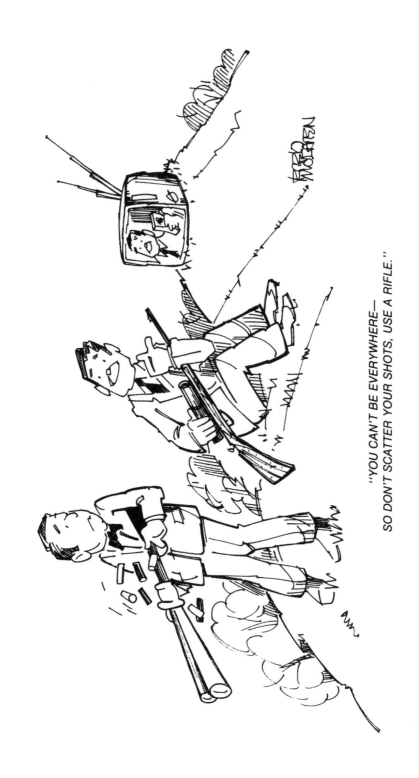

"YOU CAN'T BE EVERYWHERE—
SO DON'T SCATTER YOUR SHOTS, USE A RIFLE."

10 percent for promotion to get the business off to a good start and build identification.

It is imperative to spend your advertising dollars wisely. You can waste a lot of money before you hit on the right approach; it is therefore suggested that you find a small advertising agency to help with your campaign. A professional can give you some guidelines on your market and where your advertising dollar would be most effectively spent. And of course he/she can suggest layouts, designs and copy that will create a professional and favorable image for your product or service.

There are many media in which you can advertise. The most commonly used:

• **Newspapers.** Since so many people read a newspaper, a small, well-worded ad there can be effective. Further, if you are offering a unique product or service or have an unusual story to tell, try to interest the editorial staff in doing a feature about you and your business.

• **Radio.** Particularly in all of today's sprawling megalopolises that involve long commutes to work (Los Angeles, for example), radio has enjoyed a major revival in popularity. It therefore can be a very effective venue for advertising. Stations will often work with you in composing copy for a spot.

• **Television.** Network television commercials are prohibitively expensive. But local cable channels—especially the public access ones—offer some affordable rates for ads directed to a smaller target audience.

• **Magazines and national publications.** Here again, the trick is finding a magazine with rates you can afford. Many magazines offer classified-type advertising or small display ads. And a large magazine's regional pages may even be affordable for you. If you think a certain magazine would reach your intended audience, call and ask for a rate card.

• **Local publications.** Most communities have locally targeted publications that are highly effective if you are trying to reach a small-area audience.

• **Billboards.** Billboards are not the most effective advertising method for small businesses, though as your business grows they might be excellent supplements. Meanwhile, be aware of the most important billboard of them all: the sign outside your business. Make it clearly visible from the greatest distance possible. Keep it simple, readable, attractive—and professional.

• **Car cards.** Advertising on buses and taxis can bring results for some types of businesses or services. But check the costs first and make sure they fall within your budget restrictions.

• **Direct mail.** Refer to the "The World of Mail Order" chapter in this book (Page 95). Direct mail can be very effective, but it is advisable to test your product or service through other advertising media and limit the amount you spend on direct mail, at least in the beginning.

9. Word of mouth. The best advertising of all is a happy customer. It is human nature to want to share a "find." If you customers feel they have discovered a business that gives them good service and treats them right, they *will* talk about it. You may have to have a refund policy, use discounts, and, on occasion, repair an item at your own expense. But in the long run these costs will buy the most effective advertising available anywhere.

10. Miscellaneous. There are scores of other methods of advertising that you can look into as your business grows. Just a few: coupon mailers, cash-register tapes, place-mats and menu cards, maps, stationery, bumper stickers, T-shirts, hats, pins, pens and other gimmicks that carry your logo and/or the name of your business. A host of salespeople will call on you to sell you these things almost before you open your doors. Carefully measure any such item's cost against the potential return from it.

Legal Considerations

Whatever kind of advertising you do, there are legal guidelines you must follow. Here are a few suggestions from the United States Office of Consumer Affairs:

- **Warranties.** Always honor your warranties.
- **Truth in lending.** If you advertise payment terms, interest payments and the like, make sure they are accurate.
- **Truth in advertising.** If you advertise an item that originally cost $10 on sale for $5, be able to prove it did indeed originally cost $10.

In all phases of advertising, honesty is the best policy. Your advertising should also be in good taste, accurate and understandable; it should give information about use and maintenance in the clearest terms possible.

And take a rifle approach to advertising. Since you can't be everywhere at once (the shotgun approach), zero in on a specific market and hit that target squarely before moving on to another.

CHAPTER 18

Personnel Considerations

If you will need employees, you have some extra work to do. Finding good employees and maintaining a good employer-employee relationship is essential to success.

In the beginning you will probably require only part-time help. But as your business grows, you may want to hire more specialized labor full time. How can you, a small-business person, compete with large companies that provide great benefits? You can offer incentive bonuses, a chance to learn your business, part ownership, quick promotion and equal or better pay. Also, since you *know* what a valuable resource the older work is, you can recruit from this area.

Older persons have proved to be excellent employees for many reasons. Among the pluses:
- They have experience.
- They have fewer absences.
- They are more satisfied with their work.
- They are more stable.
- They are more loyal.

Also, remember that it is best not to hire friends or relatives. If they don't work out you not only lose an employee, you lose a friend and/or foster a lot of friction in the family.

AVOID HIRING RELATIVES—A MOTHER-IN-LAW MAY BE IMPOSSIBLE TO FIRE.

Getting Ready to Hire

Before you hire an employee, have the following ready for applicants to review:

- **A job analysis** that clearly summarizes what the position entails.
- **A job description** that explains the responsibilities, hours, and other details of the position.
- **Job specifications** that set forth the background, education and experience needed to handle the position.

By providing the above you let the applicant know up front what will be required of him/her. It will also help you later in the event an employee is not able to do the job satisfactorily, making it easier to pinpoint the reason for letting an employee go or to counsel an employee on his/her weak areas.

Before you interview an applicant, have him/her fill out a job application. This will give you details of the applicant's work background. Always have the prospective employee provide references. *Check them.*

Evaluate the prospect's application and résumé (if submitted). Then prepare a list of questions to ask during the interview. Besides providing answers to your questions, the interview should give you some idea of the person's goals, ambitions, potential, enthusiasm, etc. In other words, it will help you get to know the prospective employee on a more personal level.

Be very specific about wages, hours, vacation policy, probationary restrictions, and what you expect of an employee. Give the applicant a chance to ask *you* questions. Answer truthfully and directly. This is also the time to outline any incentives such as commissions, travel opportunities, educational programs, part ownership, profit-sharing, bonuses, etc.

After the Hire

Once you hire someone for a job, realize that how you treat that employee is as important as how you treat your customers. What your employee says and does in the community can reflect on your business either positively or negatively. A few tips on maintaining good employee relations:

- Take a personal—but not a meddlesome—interest in your employees.
- Encourage and seriously consider employees' ideas on how to improve business.
- Have frequent meetings and discussions with employees to keep them posted on future plans.
- If you need to correct an employee, do it privately. Criticism should be like a sandwich: one criticism placed between two compliments.
- Let your employees know you appreciate their work.
- Keep employees' jobs challenging and exciting.
- Offer new incentives to keep employee interest high.
- Continually review rules and regulations so employees know what is expected of them at all times.
- Respect your employees' opinions and needs.
- Always try to put yourself in your employees' place so you can understand their viewpoint.

A lot of responsibility comes with being an employer. Consult your insurance agent as to what you should offer to employees in terms of insurance coverage.

Giving the Government Its Due

A fact of life when you are in business and have employees is withholding tax—federal and state income. Withholding serves two purposes:

1. The governments receive money regularly.

2. Employees do not have to pay large amounts to the governments at the end of the year.

Other responsibilities you will have as an employer:

1. Social Security. You will deduct half of the regular payment from each employee and pay the other half yourself.

2. The Fair Labor Standards Act. This law provides for a minimum hourly wage. The amount rises from time to time and your state's minimum can be higher than the federal. If that is the case, you must abide by the state law. This Act also requires that hourly (but not salaried) employees be paid time-and-a-half for any hours they work in excess of 40.

3. Government regulation of working conditions. At the federal level employee safety and health are regulated by provisions of the Occupational Safety and Health Act (OSHA). Many states have agencies that administer this law within their own jurisdictions. Safety and health inspections can be made at any time. Be knowledgeable about the law and establish the highest health and safety standards possible for your employees.

4. Fair employment. There are laws that forbid discrimination in hiring, promotion, discharge, terms of employment, job application forms, help-wanted ads, employment-agency references, and union admission and dispatching based on physical handicap, race, color, creed, national origin, ancestry, sex or age.

As a small-business owner, you should be aware of all these legal requirements for both your own and your employees' benefit.

A BUSINESS WORKBOOK

Business Facts Almanac

John Steinbeck pointed out that a man rises to what's expected of him—but only when he is aware of what that is. The following pages include worksheets that will help you develop a detailed outline of what is expected of you in your planned business venture.

When you hear something, you will forget it.
When you see something, you will remember it.
But not until you do something, will you understand it.
— Chinese Proverb

You are urged to completely fill out all the workbook pages included here—preferably before you go to your banker, definitely before you open the doors of your business. You might or might not understand everything you have read in this book. But by putting your plans on paper and seeing first hand what is required, you will have a far better understanding of what will be required of you in your new entrepreneurial role.

Lease a man a garden and in time he will leave you a patch of sand. Make a man a full owner of a patch of sand and in time he will grow a garden on the land.
— Anonymous

The first person you will probably visit after consulting your accountant and lawyer and deciding to go ahead with your new business is your banker.

A banker is a fellow who offers to lend you his umbrella when it isn't raining.
                                                    —Anonymous

Cultivate your banker like a garden.
                                    —Anonymous

Remember, too, that your business plan is your blueprint for success. But it must be a living thing that you update as conditions and markets change.

Only one thing is certain about a new enterprise. It's going to turn out different from its business plan.
                    —William Congolton, venture capitalist

Now is the time to take the risk and walk toward the adventure that will be your new business.

It is only by risking from one hour to another that we live at all.
                                            —William James

Marketing Strategy

Step 1: Define pricing strategy.

In the following questions, all references to products also apply to services.

a. *How will you calculate the price for each product?*
b. *Which products' sales are most sensitive to price changes?*
c. *Which products will attract customers at sale prices?*
d. *How important is pricing in your overall marketing strategy?*
e. *What time of year will sales pricing be important?*
f. *What will your discount policies be?*
g. *What pricing policy will you use for slow-moving inventory?*

Pricing strategy:

_____

_____

_____

_____

_____

Step 2: Define promotional strategy.

a. *What advertising media will you use?*
b. *What days of the week will you use various media?*
c. *What media will you use during the various seasons of the year?*
d. *How will you display your merchandise?*

Promotional strategy:

_____

_____

_____

_____

Step 3: Define customer services.

a. *What special customer services will you offer?*
b. *What types of payment options will you offer?*
c. *How will you handle merchandise customers return?*

Customer services:

_____

_____

_____

_____

_____

Personal Financial Statement

*Many financial institutions (banks, savings & loans, etc.) will require information about your personal financial resources. The work on the next page will help you prepare a financial statement. This statement should be prepared **before** you put your personal assets into the business.*

Step 1: List assets.

Make a list of every asset you own, paid for or not. (Market value is the amount you would receive if you sold the asset for cash.)

Step 2: Figure Total Assets.

Add the figures in the column to find Total Assets.

Step 3: List liabilities.

Make a list of your liabilities (the money you owe).

Step 4: Figure Total Liabilities.

Add the figures in the column to find Total Liabilities.

Step 5: Calculate Net Worth.

Calculate your net worth as follows:
Total Assets – Total Liabilities = Net worth

Prepared as of _____

Assets:

Cash—checking accounts	$_____
Cash—savings accounts	_____
Notes (contract)—owed to you	_____
Certificates of deposit	_____
Life insurance (cash value)	_____
Securities—stocks and bonds	_____
Real estate (market value)	_____
Vehicles (market value)	_____
Individual retirement plans, etc.	_____
Other assets (specify)	_____
	_____

        TOTAL ASSETS $_____

Liabilities:

Current bills—you owe	$_____
Mortgages on real estate	_____
Loans—you owe	_____
Taxes—you owe	_____
Other liabilities (specify)	_____
	_____

        TOTAL LIABILITIES $_____

        NET WORTH $_____
        (Total assets minus total liabilities)

Sales Forecast

Forecasting sales of your product or service is the starting point for your financial projections. It is extremely important that your estimate be honest and realistic. Before completing the worksheet on the next page, you may want to review the Marketing Plan section of this book.

Step 1: Fill in the units sold for products 1, 2 and 3 for each month. Instead of different products, you may choose to use different departments, customer groups, or other factors.

Step 2: Fill in the sales per unit for products 1, 2 and 3.

Step 3: Calculate the total sales for each product (units sold times sale price per unit).

Step 4: Add the figures in each *row* to determine half-year sales per product.

Step 5: Add the *total sales* figure in each *column* to determine monthly total sales.

Step 6: Add the first-half and second-half sales figures to calculate year's total sales for all services.

Sales Forecast—Year 1

	1st	2nd	3rd	4th	5th	6th	1st Half Totals
Product 1							
Units sold	___	___	___	___	___	___	___
Sale price/unit	___	___	___	___	___	___	___
Total sales	___	___	___	___	___	___	___
Product 2							
Units sold	___	___	___	___	___	___	___
Sale price/unit	___	___	___	___	___	___	___
Total sales	___	___	___	___	___	___	___
Product 3							
Units sold	___	___	___	___	___	___	___
Sale price/unit	___	___	___	___	___	___	___
Total sales	___	___	___	___	___	___	___
1st-half sales all products	___	___	___	___	___	___	___

	7th	8th	9th	10th	11th	12th	2nd Half Totals
Product 1							
Units sold	____	____	____	____	____	____	____
Sale price/unit	____	____	____	____	____	____	____
Total sales	____	____	____	____	____	____	____
Product 2							
Units sold	____	____	____	____	____	____	____
Sale price/unit	____	____	____	____	____	____	____
Total sales	____	____	____	____	____	____	____
Product 3							
Units sold	____	____	____	____	____	____	____
Sale price/unit	____	____	____	____	____	____	____
Total sales	____	____	____	____	____	____	____
2nd-half sales all products	____	____	____	____	____	____	____
YEAR'S SALES ALL PRODUCTS	____	____	____	____	____	____	____

Cost of Goods Sold

In the previous section your forecast the sales of each product or service by month. Now you will be able to compute your cost for the products you will sell. For example: You might sell a product for $50, but your wholesale cost for that product might be $30, including freight.

If your business sells service only, you will not have the costs of goods sold. However, you should be able to cost out the hourly wage you pay or earn and retail the wage from there. If not, you do not need to complete this section and can go on to the worksheet on Operating Expenses—Labor-Related.

To complete this worksheet, use data from the previous worksheet (Sales Forecast).

Step 1: Calculate number of units sold.

Fill in the units sold for products 1, 2 and 3 for each month.

Step 2: Calculate cost per unit.

Fill in your cost per unit for products 1, 2 and 3.

Step 3: Calculate product cost.

Calculate the total cost for each of the products—units sold times cost per unit.

Step 4: Determine half-year cost.

Add the figures in each row to determine half-year cost per product.

Step 5: Determine monthly costs.

Add the total cost *figures in each* column *to determine monthly total costs.*

Step 6: Calculate total cost.

Add the first half and second-half cost figures to calculate year's total cost for all products.

Cost of Goods Sold—Year 1

	1st	2nd	3rd	4th	5th	6th	1st Half Totals
Product 1							
Units sold	——	——	——	——	——	——	——
Cost/unit	——	——	——	——	——	——	——
Total cost	——	——	——	——	——	——	——
Product 2							
Units sold	——	——	——	——	——	——	——
Cost/unit	——	——	——	——	——	——	——
Total cost	——	——	——	——	——	——	——
Product 3							
Units sold	——	——	——	——	——	——	——
Cost/unit	——	——	——	——	——	——	——
Total cost	——	——	——	——	——	——	——
1st-half cost all products	——	——	——	——	——	——	——

	7th	8th	9th	10th	11th	12th	2nd Half Totals
Product 1							
Units sold	___	___	___	___	___	___	___
Cost/unit	___	___	___	___	___	___	___
Total cost	___	___	___	___	___	___	___
Product 2							
Units sold	___	___	___	___	___	___	___
Cost/unit	___	___	___	___	___	___	___
Total cost	___	___	___	___	___	___	___
Product 3							
Units sold	___	___	___	___	___	___	___
Cost/unit	___	___	___	___	___	___	___
Total cost	___	___	___	___	___	___	___
2nd-half cost all products	___	___	___	___	___	___	___
YEAR'S COST ALL PRODUCTS	___	___	___	___	___	___	___

Operating Expense—Labor

*Labor is your first major category of operating expense. In this section you will calculate the **total cost** of having employees working for your business. This total includes wages and salaries, payroll taxes required by law, and optional fringe benefits you provide.*

Step 1:

Write the title of each employee.

Step 2:

Fill in each employee's salary or wage for each month.

Step 3:

Add the figures in each row to determine half-year salaries for each position.

Step 4:

*Add the figures in each column to determine the total monthly **salaries**.*

Step 5:

*Calculate the three types of **payroll taxes** for each of the 12 months. Repeat steps 3 and 4.*

Step 6:

*List and calculate the **optional employee benefits** (e.g., medical/dental insurance, life insurance, pension plan payments, incentive bonuses, etc.) for each of the 12 months. Repeat steps 3 and 4.*

Step 7:

*Calculate the **total** labor-related expenses for each month.*

Labor Expenses—Year 1

Salary per month Position	1st	2nd	3rd	4th	5th	6th	1st Half Totals
1. _____	___	___	___	___	___	___	___
2. _____	___	___	___	___	___	___	___
3. _____	___	___	___	___	___	___	___
4. _____	___	___	___	___	___	___	___
Total	___	___	___	___	___	___	___
Payroll taxes Employer portion Social Security	___	___	___	___	___	___	___
Federal/state	___	___	___	___	___	___	___
Workers' compensation insurance	___	___	___	___	___	___	___
Total	___	___	___	___	___	___	___
Optional employee benefits Medical/dental insurance	___	___	___	___	___	___	___
Other benefits	___	___	___	___	___	___	___
	___	___	___	___	___	___	___
TOTAL	___	___	___	___	___	___	___

Salary per month Position	1st Half Carried	7th	8th	9th	10th	11th	12th	Year's Totals
1. _____	_____	___	___	___	___	___	___	_____
2. _____	_____	___	___	___	___	___	___	_____
3. _____	_____	___	___	___	___	___	___	_____
4. _____	_____	___	___	___	___	___	___	_____
Total	_____	___	___	___	___	___	___	_____

Payroll taxes
Employer portion

Social Security	_____	___	___	___	___	___	___	_____
Federal/state	_____	___	___	___	___	___	___	_____
Workers' compensation insurance	_____	___	___	___	___	___	___	_____
Total	_____	___	___	___	___	___	___	_____

Optional employee benefits

Medical/dental insurance	_____	___	___	___	___	___	___	_____
Other benefits	_____	___	___	___	___	___	___	_____
TOTAL	_____	___	___	___	___	___	___	_____

Nonlabor Expenses

Operating a business involves a wide variety of nonlabor expenses. Many are referred to as overhead, which means they are fixed—they will remain constant regardless of sales. Two examples of fixed expenses are utilities and insurance premiums.

On the other hand, some expenses do rise or fall as sales increase or decrease. These are variable expenses. An example might be car/ delivery expense: As sales rise, delivery expense will probably increase.

Step 1:

Review the expenses listed on the facing page. You may have some expenses not listed here; write them in the "other" spaces.

Step 2:

Fill in your monthly estimate for each category of expense. Remember that some will vary through the year, especially if your business is seasonal.

Step 3:

Calculate total expenses for each month—add the figures in each row.

Step 4:

Calculate yearly totals for each expense—add the figures in each column.

Nonlabor Expenses—Year 1

	1st	2nd	3rd	4th	5th	6th	1st Half Total
Rent	____	____	____	____	____	____	____
Utilities	____	____	____	____	____	____	____
Car/delivery	____	____	____	____	____	____	____
Supplies	____	____	____	____	____	____	____
Advertising	____	____	____	____	____	____	____
Legal/accounting	____	____	____	____	____	____	____
Insurance	____	____	____	____	____	____	____
Bad debts	____	____	____	____	____	____	____
Interest	____	____	____	____	____	____	____
Other	____	____	____	____	____	____	____
Depreciation	____	____	____	____	____	____	____

(Leave this line blank for now)

	1st	2nd	3rd	4th	5th	6th	1st Half Total
TOTAL	____	____	____	____	____	____	____

	1st Half Carried	7th	8th	9th	10th	11th	12th	Year's Total
Rent	_____	___	___	___	___	___	___	_____
Utilities	_____	___	___	___	___	___	___	_____
Car/delivery	_____	___	___	___	___	___	___	_____
Supplies	_____	___	___	___	___	___	___	_____
Advertising	_____	___	___	___	___	___	___	_____
Legal/accounting	_____	___	___	___	___	___	___	_____
Insurance	_____	___	___	___	___	___	___	_____
Bad debts	_____	___	___	___	___	___	___	_____
Interest	_____	___	___	___	___	___	___	_____
Other	_____	___	___	___	___	___	___	_____
Depreciation	_____	___	___	___	___	___	___	_____

(Leave this line blank for now)

TOTAL	_____	___	___	___	___	___	___	_____

Capital Equipment

This section will help you plan purchases of capital equipment needed to start your business. Capital equipment includes machines, display cases, office furniture, computers, vehicles, and any other asset with a useful life of more than one year.

This section will also help you calculate the monthly depreciation for each capital asset. Depreciation is the original cost of a piece of equipment divided by its useful life in months. For example, if a truck costs $6,000 and has a useful life of five years (60 months), its monthly depreciation is $100.

Step 1:

List each item of equipment needed to start your business.

Step 2:

Fill in the cost required to buy each piece of equipment (new or used).

Step 3:

Estimate the useful life (in months) of each piece of equipment.

Step 4:

Fill in the monthly depreciation for each piece of equipment.

Step 5:

Calculate the totals for capital equipment and monthly depreciation.

Capital Equipment Depreciation

Equipment	Cost	New or Used?	Useful Life (in Months)	Monthly Depreciation
_____	$_____	_____	_____	$_____
_____	_____	_____	_____	_____
_____	_____	_____	_____	_____
_____	_____	_____	_____	_____
_____	_____	_____	_____	_____
_____	_____	_____	_____	_____
_____	_____	_____	_____	_____
_____	_____	_____	_____	_____
_____	_____	_____	_____	_____
_____	_____	_____	_____	_____
_____	_____	_____	_____	_____
_____	_____	_____	_____	_____
_____	_____	_____	_____	_____
_____	_____	_____	_____	_____

TOTAL COST
CAPITAL EQUIPMENT $_____

TOTAL MONTHLY
DEPRECIATION $_____

Start-Up Expenses

Start-up expenses are those it will take to open your doors for business. Some will be one-time expenditures, others will be periodic.

Step 1:

Review the expenses listed on these two pages. You may have additional costs that are not listed; write them under other expenses.

Step 2:

Estimate your cost for each item.

Step 3:

Calculate your total start-up expenses.

Expense	Cost
Total cost of capital equipment (from page 193)	_____
Beginning inventory (for retail business)	_____
Supplies (office, etc.)	_____
Legal fees	_____
Accounting fees	_____
Licenses and permits	_____
Remodeling	_____
Deposits (utilities, etc.)	_____
Advertising (grand opening)	_____
Promotion (door prizes, etc.)	_____
Other expenses:	_____
_____	_____
_____	_____
TOTAL START-UP EXPENSES	$_____

Projected Income Statement—Year 1

You are now ready to assemble the data for your projected income statement. This will calculate your net profit or loss (before income taxes) for each month.

Step 1:

Fill in your monthly sales figures from pages 180–181.

Step 2:

Fill in your monthly cost-of-goods-sold figures from pages 184–185.

Step 3:

Calculate the gross margin for each month (Sales minus cost of goods sold).

Step 4:

Fill in your monthly labor-expense figures from pages 187–188.

Step 5:

Fill in your monthly nonlabor-expense figures from pages 190–191.

Step 6:

Fill your monthly depreciation figures from page 193.

Step 7:

Calculate the total operating expense for each month.

Step 8:

Calculate the net profit or loss (before income taxes) for each month (gross margin minus total operating expenses).

Projected Income—Year 1 by Month

	1st	2nd	3rd	4th	5th	6th	7th	8th	9th	10th	11th	12th	Year's Total
Sales													
Cost of goods													
Gross margin													
Operating expenses													
Salaries													
Payroll taxes													
Employee benefits													
Rent													
Utilities													
Car/delivery													
Supplies													
Advertising													
Legal/accounting													
Insurance													
Bad debts													
Interest													
Other													
Depreciation													
Total operating expense													
NET PROFIT (OR LOSS) BEFORE INCOME TAXES													

Projected Income—Years 2 and 3 by Quarter

*On page 196 you completed an income statement for **year 1** of your operation. In this section you will complete statements for **years 2 and 3**, but by quarters rather than months.*

Step 1:

Fill in the sales for each quarter using figures from pages 180–181.

Step 2:

Fill in the cost of goods sold for each quarter using figures from pages 184–185.

Step 3:

Calculate the gross margin for each quarter (sales minus cost of goods sold).

Step 4:

Fill in your quarterly labor-expense figures from pages 187–188.

Step 5:

Fill in your quarterly nonlabor-expense figures from pages 190–191.

Step 6:

Fill in your quarterly depreciation expense using figures from page 193.

Step 7:

Calculate the total operating expense for each quarter.

Step 8:

Calculate the net profit or loss (gross margin minus total operating expenses) before income taxes for each quarter.

Projected Income—Years 2 and 3 Worksheet

	1st	2nd	3rd	4th	Total Year 2	1st	2nd	3rd	4th	Total Year 3
Sales										
Cost of goods										
Gross margin										
Operating expenses										
Salaries										
Payroll taxes										
Employee benefits										
Rent										
Utilities										
Car/delivery										
Supplies										
Advertising										
Legal/accounting										
Insurance										
Bad debts										
Interest										
Other										
Depreciation										
Total operating expense										
NET PROFIT (OR LOSS) BEFORE INCOME TAXES										

Projected Cash Flow—Year 1
by Month

Cash-flow projections are among the most critical you will make. You will calculate your cash receipts and cash disbursements for each month. If receipts are greater than disbursements, you will have a **positive cash flow**. *If receipts are less than disbursements, you will have a* **negative flow**. *Negative cash flows are put in brackets; e.g., [$5,218].*

Step 1:

Fill in your beginning cash balance for the first month.

Step 2:

Fill in the various categories of cash receipts for the first month only.

Step 3:

Fill in the various categories of cash disbursements and total them for the first month only.

Step 4:

Calculate the net flow balance for the first month (total cash receipts minus total cash disbursements).

Step 5:

Calculate the ending cash balance for the first month (beginning cash balance plus a positive net cash flow).

Step 6:

Fill in the beginning cash balance for the second month (the ending cash balance for the first month).

Step 7:

Repeat the first six steps for each month, one month at a time.

Projected Cash Flow—Year 1 Worksheet

	1st	2nd	3rd	4th	5th	6th	7th	8th	9th	10th	11th	12th
Beginning cash balance												
Cash receipts												
Cash sales												
Collect accounts receivable												
Bank loans, etc.												
Other receipts												
Total cash receipts												
Cash disbursements												
Product purchases												
Salaries												
Payroll tax/fringes												
Rent												
Utilities												
Interest												
Other:_____												
Purchase capital equipment												
Loan principal pymt.												
Owner's draw												
Total cash spent												
Net cash flow												
ENDING CASH BALANCE												

Projected Cash Flow—Years 2 and 3 by Quarter

*You have now completed the cash flow projections for **year 1** of your operation. In this section you will complete the cash-flow projections for **years 2** and **3**, but by quarter. Follow the same seven steps listed on pages 196 and 198, completing one quarter at a time.*

Projected Cash Flow—Years 2 and 3 Worksheet

	1st	2nd	3rd	4th	1st	2nd	3rd	4th
Beginning cash balance								
Cash receipts								
Cash sales								
Collect accounts receivable								
Bank loans, etc.								
Other receipts								
Total cash receipts								
Cash disbursements								
Product purchases								
Salaries								
Payroll tax/fringes								
Rent								
Utilities								
Interest								
Other:								
Purchase capital equipment								
Loan principal pymt.								
Owner's draw								
Total cash spent								
Net cash flow								
ENDING CASH BALANCE								

Sources and Uses of Financing

*This section is another critical financial forecast: What will be the **sources** of your initial financing? Then, how will you **use** this financing to buy the assets needed to open your doors for business?*

Step 1:

Fill in the cash amounts to be invested by the various owners.

Step 2:

Fill in the market value of the noncash assets (e.g., equipment, vehicles, buildings) to be invested by the various owners.

Step 3:

Fill in the amounts of bank loans to your business, both short-term (one year or less) and long-term.

Step 4:

Fill in the amounts of personal loans that will probably be secured by your personal assets (e.g., your home).

Step 5:

Fill in any Small Business Administration-guaranteed loans, and loans from any other sources.

Step 6:

Fill in the amounts of cash that will be used to buy various assets in the uses of financing section.

Step 7:

Fill in the value of noncash assets contributed by the owners (as listed in the sources of financing section).

Step 8:

Total both sources and uses sections: They should be equal.

Sources of financing:

Investment of cash by owner 1	$ _____
Investment of cash by owner 2	_____
Investment of noncash assets by owner 1	_____
Investment of noncash assets by owner 2	_____
Bank loans to business—short-term	_____
Bank loans to business—long-term	_____
Bank loans—personal	_____
Small Business Administration-guaranteed loans	_____
Others (specify)	_____
TOTAL SOURCES OF FINANCING	$ _____

Uses of financing:

Land $ _____

Buildings   _____

Equipment   _____

Remodeling   _____

Beginning inventory   _____

Working capital to pay operating expenses   _____

Noncash assets contributed by owners
  (same figure as in sources)   _____

TOTAL USES OF FINANCING $ _____

Balance Sheet

*The balance sheet is a picture of your financial condition on a **particular** day. It is an inventory of your assets (at your cost), your liabilities (debts), and your equity in the assets.*

*You need to prepare a balance sheet at the **start-up** of your business. Include the assets and liabilities as of the day you open the doors.*

Step 1:

Fill in the amount for each current asset and add the figures to get total current assets.

Step 2:

Fill in the amount for each fixed asset—land, buildings and equipment—using the prices you paid for them.

Step 3:

Put a zero (0) on the line for accumulated depreciation below both buildings and equipment. The book value is the cost minus the accumulated depreciation. Now calculate total fixed assets.

Step 4:

Calculate total assets by adding total current assets and total fixed assets.

Step 5:

Fill in the amount for each liability. Calculate total current liabilities and total long-term liabilities, then add those two figures to determine total liabilities.

Step 6:

Calculate the owner's equity by subtracting total liabilities from total assets.

Step 7:

Add total liabilities and owner's equity. This figure should equal the figure for total assets.

Balance Sheet Worksheet

Prepared as of: _____

Assets

Current assets

Accounts receivable $_____

Inventory   _____

Prepaid expenses   _____

Other current assets   _____

   Total current assets $_____

Fixed assets

Land   _____

Buildings $_____

Less accumulated depreciation   _____

   Book value—buildings   _____

Equipment   _____

Less accumulated depreciation   _____

   Book value—equipment   _____

Other fixed assets   _____

   Total fixed assets $_____

Total assets $_____

Liabilities

Current liabilities

Accounts payable $_____

Federal & state taxes owed   _____

Other current liabilities   _____

    Total current liabilities $_____

Long-term liabilities

Notes payable to bank $_____

Mortgages payable   _____

Other long-term liabilities   _____

    Total long-term liabilities $_____

Total liabilities $_____

Owner's equity (total assets minus total liabilities) $_____

TOTAL LIABILITIES + OWNER'S EQUITY $_____

Break-Even Analysis

The break-even point is where total sales exactly cover total costs and operating expenses. This level of sales is the break-even-point sales level (BEP sales).

In other words, at the BEP sales level you make zero profit. If you sell more than the BEP sales level, you make a net profit. If you sell less than the BEP sales level, you sustain a net loss.

The worksheet that follows will calculate your BEP sales level for any year of operation. The steps assume that you are calculating the BEP sales level for year 1. But costs and expenses will change as your business continues, so monitor your BEP regularly.

Step 1:

Fill in the figures for total sales, total cost of goods sold and total gross margin for year 1 from the projected income statement for year 1 on page 197.

Step 2:

Calculate the gross margin percentage as directed on the worksheet. Gross margin percentage tells you what percentage of each dollar of sales results in gross margin.

Step 3:

Fill in the figure for total start-up expenses from page 195.

Step 4:

Calculate the BEP sales level as directed on the worksheet. You need to reach this level of sales to break even.

Break-Even Worksheet

Total sales $ _____

Total cost of goods sold $ _____

Total gross margin $ _____

Gross profit % $\dfrac{\text{Total gross margin}}{\text{Total sales}}$ = $\begin{array}{l}\text{\$ _____}\\[4pt]\text{\$ _____}\end{array}$

Gross margin % 0. _____
(Leave the gross margin % as a decimal; i.e., 0.347, not 34.7%.)

Total operating expenses $ _____

BEP sales level $\dfrac{\text{Total operating expenses}}{\text{Gross margin \%}}$ = $\begin{array}{l}\text{\$ _____}\\[4pt]\text{0. _____}\end{array}$

BEP SALES
LEVEL $_____

Timetable

You will need to amend your timetable periodically as you progress through this workbook. The purpose is to assure that activities vital to the success of your business are identified and completed. (This worksheet can be a great help in all manner of things, incidentally, such as planning the annual family reunion!)

Step 1: Identify Key Activities.

Review other portions of your business plan to compile a list of key activities.

Step 2: Assign responsibility for each activity.

For each identified activity, assign one person who will be primarily responsible for its completion.

Step 3: Determine scheduled start date.

For each activity, determine the date when work will begin. Consider how the activity fits into your overall plan as well as the availability of the person responsible.

Step 4: Determine scheduled finish date.

For each activity, determine when the activity must be completed.

Activity	Responsible Person	Start Date	Finish Date

Summary

Step 1: Verify completion of previous pages.

Finish all previous sections in the workbook before proceeding.

Step 2: Identify your business plan's audience.

Just who do you want to satisfy with this business plan? The summary should briefly address all issues important to that person and probably be the first page he or she reads. Again, it is extremely important that the summary be brief, yet contain the information most important to the reader. It should make its audience want to read the rest of your plan.

Step 3: Write a one-page summary.

You will now need to tighten your writing style because you want to write no more than one page summarizing all the worksheets you have completed!

Determine which sections are going to be of greatest interest to your reader. Write one to three sentences summarizing each of the important sections.

These sentences should appear in the same order as the sections of your business plan. And the watchword is continuity: The sentences should flow together to form a summary, not be a group of loosely related thoughts.

You may want to prepare several different summaries, depending on who you will be presenting your business plan to.

Supporting Exhibits

Step 1: Identify desired supporting exhibits.

Using the checklist, identify documents you will be using as supporting exhibits for your business plan.

Step 2: Collect supporting exhibits.

Complete any documents that are not readily available and obtain copies of those that already exist. Use the checklist to keep track of exhibits you have gathered and those that must be assembled.

Exhibit	Needed?	Completed?
Historical financial statements	_____	_____
Tax returns	_____	_____
Résumés	_____	_____
Organizational chart	_____	_____
Floor layout	_____	_____
Map showing location	_____	_____
Job descriptions	_____	_____
Legal documents	_____	_____
Credit reports	_____	_____
Patents	_____	_____
Letters of reference	_____	_____
Photos of business	_____	_____
Bills of materials	_____	_____
Routing slips	_____	_____
Market survey report	_____	_____

Checklist for Starting a New Business

☐ 1. **Registration of an assumed business name:** Register an assumed business name with the Department of Commerce, your county or city clerk's office, etc.

☐ 2. **State/local occupation permits and/or licenses:** You may need to apply for the privilege of engaging in certain professions, trades, businesses or occupations with state and/or local agencies.

☐ 3. **Employer's application for identification number:** Apply for this identification number at an Internal Revenue Service office or Social Security office.

☐ 4. **City business license:** Apply at your city hall if business and/or occupation taxes are levied.

☐ 5. **State withholding tax return:** File these returns with your state's taxing agency.

☐ 6. **State sales tax return:** Depending on which state your business will be located and what type of business you have, apply and collect reporting forms and understand procedures involving state taxes from your state's taxing agency.

☐ 7. **Status report:** File this report to determine your liability for contributions to unemployment compensation with your state's employment division.

☐ 8. **Employer's written application to state compensation department:** This application is for those employers who have other than "direct responsibility."

☐ **9. Occupational Safety and Health Administration (OSHA):** Contact this federal agency to determine if there are regulations that apply to your business. Contact the accident prevention division of your state's workers' compensation agency.

☐ **10. State environmental agency:** You may need to check regulations involving water, air and noise pollution.

☐ **11. Legal concerns:** Consult an attorney regarding your form of business ownership, leases, contacts, etc.

☐ **12. Accounting concerns:** Consult an accountant regarding bookkeeping systems, income tax planning, income tax returns, payroll reports and similar items.

☐ **13. Insurance concerns:** Consult an insurance agent about various forms of insurance: fire, automobile, employee health and life, fidelity (insuring your business against employee theft), burglary and vandalism, business interruption, and key-employee insurance.

☐ **14. Banking concerns:** Consult a banker about establishing a line of credit, checking accounts, future borrowing requirements, and other concerns.

☐ **15. Trade associations:** Contact these for helpful information about starting your business.

☐ **16. Chamber of Commerce:** Contact your local chamber regarding its helpful services to new businesses in the community.

☐ **17. Economic development agencies:** You may want to contact your city, county or state for resources to help you start your business.

☐ **18. Small-business development centers:** You may want to contact one of these centers for assistance in starting your business.

Epilogue

You have just completed, or are about to complete, the first two quarters of your life. The fact is, you are on the threshold of what can be in many, many ways the *best* years of your life.

You are uniquely qualified to start and run a business of your own. During the first half of life you amassed the knowledge, experience, skills and confidence that give you the competitive edge. All of this adds up to this age-plus factor.

The purpose of this book is to convince you that armed with the age-plus factor, you are exceptionally well qualified and have a high probability of succeeding in business.

But this book offers much more than the tools to help you organize and run your own business. Although there have been a great number of books written on the subject of organizing a small business, few have been targeted to people over 50.

In Part I we invited you to take a look at yourself: to assess and inventory your skills, strengths and talents; to discover that you are materially, psychologically and emotionally highly qualified, that your accumulated experience is transferable to a new and successful business, and that all of this will help you successfully meet the challenge of forgoing the status quo to find your own fulfillment and pleasure. And we hope we proved to you that the past is only prologue to the future.

You have learned to connect to other people and realize that

one of your most valuable assets is the network you've been building and nurturing all these years—the network of people who can
help you succeed. You now realize that your personal research,
development and education do not stop, but are lifelong. Either
through crisis or through choice, you have developed a positive
attitude and confidence that will see you through this great venture.

Once you have evaluated your strengths and weaknesses you
can match yourself to a business that fits your abilities and rely on
yourself to bring into being an enterprise that will provide the challenge, satisfaction and fun that will so enrich the second half of your
life.

Of course you *can* choose the security route for the many years
ahead. But wouldn't you be better off calculating the odds and taking a risk—a calculated risk? In our chapter "Preparing for Risk"
our premise is that if you adequately prepare yourself, you maxi-
mize your chances of success and minimize the possibility of failure.
We believe risk is really worth its cost because with risk come
growth, new experiences, feelings of accomplishment, new knowledge, fullness of life, and a chance to realize a lifetime of dreams.

In Part II we help you bridge the gap between your ammuni-
tion and your target. We try to guide you in creating a road map for
the second half of life that matches your skills to the types of businesses that will suit you best and therefore be the most fulfilling.

Your research will lead you to a business that fits your background, experience and personality, whether it be through buying
a franchise, marketing your own product, offering mail-order merchandise, developing a needed service, starting a business at home,
or buying an existing business that appeals to you.

You have within you the spark of creativity required to build
your own business. Thomas Edison did it by harnessing electricity.
Henry Ford by perfecting the assembly line. But lesser known people developed Velcro, figured out how to use pressed popcorn to
prevent breakage in packaging, conceived the idea that a rock could

be marketed as the perfect pet, and, more recently invented Post-its by accident!

In Part III we explained the nuts and bolts all businesses must use in structuring their operations. We can't put these tools in place for you, however; only *you* can do that.

We outlined all the homework you must do before you actually open the door. And the Appendix lists many resource books that can be of great help.

You have worked eight hours a day for others. You will work many more hours than that now—but you will be the boss, working for yourself. Many of us will work *12* hours for ourselves and it seems a much shorter time because it is *our* choice to do so. Doing the financing, the bookkeeping, the marketing and promotion, the servicing and supplying, the hiring and firing—and yes, even sweeping the floor—can give you great satisfaction and make this the most exciting time of your life—because it all belongs to you.

So do your homework, calculate the odds, follow through, make a commitment to your goal, your plan and yourself—and GO FOR IT!

References

Small Business Information Sources

The Institute for Success Over 50, Albert Myers, President, PO Box 160, Aspen, CO 81612; (303) 925-1900

Small Business Administration, 1441 L St NW, Rm 100, Washington, DC 20416; (202) 205-6600

Business Plans

Small Business Administration
   Business Plan for Retailers MA2002
   Business Plan for Small Construction MA2008
   Business Plan for Small Manufacturers MA2007
   Box 15434, Fort Worth, TX 76119

Understanding Financial Statements

The Centre for Entrepreneurial Management, 311 Main St, Worcester, MA 01608; (617) 755-0770

The Entrepreneur Handbook

Merrill Lynch Pierce Fenner & Smith (contact local office)

Entrepreneurial Education

Small Business Development Center: Call (202) 205-6766 for information on the center in your state.

Regional SBA offices:

Boston: (617) 565-5590
New York: (212) 264-7772
Philadelphia: (215) 962-3816
Atlanta: (404) 347-2441
Chicago: (312) 353-0359
Dallas: (214) 767-7643
Kansas City: (816) 374-6757
Denver: (303) 534-7518
San Francisco: (415) 556-7487
Seattle: (206) 442-5676

Resource Organizations Serving Small Business

Center for Small Business, Chamber of Commerce of the United States, 1615 H St NW, Washington, DC 20062; (202) 659-6000

COSIBA: The Council of Small and Independent Business Associations is a federation of eight regional small-business associations

Council of Smaller Enterprises of the Greater Cleveland Growth Association, 690 Union Commerce Bldg, Cleveland, OH 44115; (216) 621-3300

Independent Business Association of Wisconsin, 415 E Washington Ave, Madison, WI 53703; (608) 251-5546

National Association of Small Business Investment Companies, 512 Washington Bldg, Washington, DC 20011; (202) 824-5900

National Federal of Independent Business, 490 L'Enfant Plaza SW, Washington, DC 20006; (202) 554-9000

National Federation of Independent Business, 150 W 20th Ave, San Mateo, CA 94402; (415) 341-7441

National Small Business Association, 1604 K St NW, Washington, DC 20006; (202) 293-8830

National Small Business Association of New England, 69 Hickory Dr, Waltham, MA 02154; (617) 840-9070

Smaller Manufacturer's Council, 339 Boulevard of Allies, Pittsburgh, PA 15222; (412) 391-1622

Small Business Financial Aids

Commercial Credit Corporation, 300 St. Paul Pl, Baltimore, MD 21202; (301) 332-3000

Control Data Business Centers are rapidly expanding around the country, offering data processing services, business planning and marketing assistance, a full range of lending services, and more:

Atlanta: 300 Embasy Row, 6600 Peachtree-Dunwoody Rd, Atlanta, GA 30328; (404) 399-2170

Baltimore: PO Box 549, 22 W Padonia Rd, Ste C-152, Timonium, MD 21093; (301) 561-1800

Charlotte: PO Box 34189, 3726 Latrobe Dr, Ste 101, Charlotte, NC 28234; (704) 365-1420

Chicago: Business Centre, 2001 Midwest Rd, Suite 105, Oak Brook, IL 60521; (312) 629-7991

Cleveland: Business Center, Western Reserve Bldg, 1468 W 9th St, Ste 100, Cleveland, OH 44113; (216) 523-1510

Dallas: Control Data Building, 14801 Quorum Dr, Ste 200, Dallas, TX 7524?; (214) 385-5750

Denver: 7100 East Belleview Ave, Ste 200, Englewood, CO 80111; (303) 779-2900

Kansas City: Executive Hills Office Park, 11011 Antioch, Overland Park, KS 66210; (913) 648-1422

Los Angeles: 18831 Con Karman Ave, Ste 300, Irvine, CA 92715; (714) 851-5620

Louisville: 10200 Linn Station Rd, Triad E, Ste 150, Louisville, KY 40223; (502) 423-1660

Minneapolis: 5241 Viking Dr, Bloomington, MN 55425; (612) 893-4200

New York: 1350 Avenue of the Americas, New York, NY 10019; (212) 887-1010

San Francisco: 1350 Old Bayshore Hwy, One Bay Plaza, Ste 330, Burlingame, CA 94010; (415) 342-7622

Tampa: 4511 N Himes Ave, Business Center, Ste 285, Tampa, FL 33614; (818) 877-5523

Entrepreneurial Seminars

The Country Business Brokers, 225 Main St, Brattleboro, VT 05301;
(802) 254-4504. Fee $260

The Entrepreneurship Institute, 909 E Wilson Bridge Rd, Ste 247, Worthington, OH 43085; (614) 885-0585. Fee: $300

Marshall Thurber Enterprises, 1700 Montgomery, Ste 230, San Francisco,
CA 94111

Franchise Listings

Directory of Franchising Organizations, Pilot Industries, 103 Cooper St,
New York, NY 11702. $3.95

The Franchise Annual, Info Press Inc., 736 Center St, Lewiston, NY 14902;
(716) 754-4669

Patents and Trademarks

Small Business Administration, 1441 L St NW, Washington, DC 20005

Small Business Administration, SBIC Division, 1441 L St NW, Washington, DC 20005

Professional Help

American Bar Association, 1155 E 60th St, Chicago, IL 60637

Martanindale-Hubbell Law Directory (at local library)

Graphics & Printing

Check local Yellow Pages for graphic artists and printers

Tax Information

IRS Publication 334, Tax Guide to Small Business, U.S. Government
Printing Office, North Capitol and H Sts, Washington, DC 20401

Women Entrepreneurs

American Women's Economic Development Corporation, 250 Broadway, New York, NY 10007

National Association of Women Business Owners, 600 S Federal, Chicago, IL 60605; (312) 922–0465

WHERE DO I GO FROM HERE?

For a personal analysis of your background and talents, THE INSTITUTE FOR SUCCESS OVER 50 will assist you in determining the business or career best suited for you.

Send us the results of the **personal profile** *Should I Go Into Business for Myself?* on page 2 along with any other pertinent information you may have and $25. The Institute will analyze your background and send you a CUSTOMIZED LIST of recommendations.

You will also receive research material on the OVER FIFTY MARKET:

- Information as to the companies and industries that hire people over 50.
- Information on franchises that would work for you.
- Information and tips on the specific business you are interested in.
- Information on how to get started.

Get Started Today

Send $25 along with your name and address to:

INSTITUTE FOR SUCCESS OVER 50
''Blueprint for Success''
BOX 160 Dept N
ASPEN, CO 81612

Introducing our new series of Newcastle originals: the Looking Forward Collection. This creative line of books will provide solid, comprehensive information and advice for people over 50 on lifestyle, finances, relationships, health and fitness, careers, housing, retirement, and much, much more.